D1191547

THE HORSE AND BUGGY AGE
IN NEW ENGLAND

THE
HORSE & BUGGY AGE
IN NEW ENGLAND
Edwin Valentine Mitchell

GRYPHON BOOKS
ANN ARBOR, MICHIGAN · 1971

This is a facsimile reprint of the
1937 edition published in New York
by Coward - McCann, Inc.

Library of Congress Catalog Card Number 70–143637

To

EMLYN VALENTINE MITCHELL

1854-1934

CONTENTS

CONTENTS

THE HORSE AND BUGGY AGE

CHAPTER I

The Horse and Buggy Age

IN THE horse and buggy age the finest privately owned vehicle in the New England city where I live was Charles Dillon's hearse. This hearse was a reduced replica of Grant's Tomb. Drawn by a perfectly matched pair of coal-black horses, people used to turn and gaze with admiration at the mobile mausoleum as it rolled slowly down the street bound for one or another of our cemeteries.

Always conservative, New England was one of the last sections of the country to go over to motorized funerals. There seemed to be something irreverent and undignified in speeding the departed on their way in a horseless hearse. As late as 1913, when the body of J. P. Morgan the elder was brought to his native city of Hartford, Connecticut, for burial, his funeral cortège was composed of a horse-drawn hearse and a long line of solemn hacks. At that time the horse, which had played such an important part in our history, had for several years been on its last legs. The Morgan funeral definitely marked the end of the equine era.

Even then people did not seem to realize how completely the horse was to disappear from the scene. For that same year, when a memorial was erected at Hartford in honor of Colonel Albert A. Pope, who as one of America's pioneer automobile manufacturers did as much as anyone to render the horse obsolescent, it took the form of a large, handsome, stone water-trough for horses. Time has written its ironical comment on this horse-trough, memorial to the bearded motor-car maker. Less than twenty-five years after its erection the fountain has become a curious relic from another civilization.

Not only horse-troughs but other relics of the horse and buggy age in New England, such as hitching-posts and carriage stones, survive here and there to remind us how far we have traveled since that age. Occasionally I even see a few English sparrows in the street, and straightway arises a memory of late winter afternoons in Boston thirty or forty years ago when the chirping of hundreds of sparrows in the ivy of the old Probate Office next to King's Chapel could be heard above the din of the traffic in Tremont Street.

The sparrow never suffered as wild birds do from the seasons. Its food supply was never wholly cut off. Snow seldom completely blocked the entrances to stables and warehouses. Nor did drought affect it. Too canny to be caught by cats, the sparrow had one serious enemy, the small boy with slingshot, air gun, or snare. Sparrow

clubs went hunting on Saturdays. Every boy knew that
Longfellow in his youth wept when he shot a robin, but
that in the death of a sparrow there was nothing for
tears. Despite the boy hunters, the sparrow multiplied
until it became a public nuisance. Its untidy nests were
everywhere—in the cornices, friezes, and porches of
buildings. It even built in the hoods of the old-fashioned
spluttering arc lights. As often as a sparrow's nest
was raked down from a niche or crevice, it cheerfully
went to work rebuilding with straw, wisps of hay, horse-
hair, and bits of string and fluff found blowing about
the streets. It was a great day for the sparrows after
the Tenth Cavalry from Fort Ethan Allen had clattered
through town on the way to summer maneuvers.

Since then the horse and buggy age has disappeared
down the road of history. Many people can remember
when it ended, but hardly a person now alive can remember when it began. It is not easy to say just when
it had its inception. One cannot point to a particular
year, month, or day and say that is when it began.
But it can be said that in point of historical time it
did not last long—no longer than the lifetime of the
average man. Speaking arbitrarily, one might say that
the horse and buggy age began in 1850 and ended in
1910, with its vintage years lying between the admin-
istrations of Lincoln and McKinley.

In some ways the horse and buggy age was not so
slow as some people may imagine. During the early
years of the period, for example, when there were no
telephones and the telegraph service was feeble and limited, the newspapers of New England gathered election

returns with astonishing speed. The *Springfield Republican* had a system of horse and buggy expresses which enabled it to collect the returns from the four western Massachusetts counties of Hampden, Hampshire, Franklin, and Berkshire before midnight. Reporters were sent out in various directions, but the one with the widest reach of country was the reporter who scoured the Berkshire Hills. This reporter had to drive nearly fifty miles after the polls closed, getting returns himself and collecting them from messengers sent from the remoter towns to meet him along the way. Then with the complete returns for Berkshire County in his pocket, he would climb into the cab of a specially chartered locomotive and return to Springfield. In the national and state election of 1852 the returns for the four counties were in the *Republican* office and being tabulated for the next morning's issue of the paper by 11 P. M.

At the Springfield railroad station the conductors in those days carried horsewhips to keep boys off the cars. Their curiosity about trains was shared by everyone. It was the Iron Horse that gave New Englanders their first taste of speed. Longfellow has told of the effect the coming of the railroad had upon many self-contained New England communities. Much of their rural quietude and solitude was destroyed. "The inhabitants became restless and ambitious. They were in constant excitement and alarm, like children in story books hidden away somewhere by an ogre, who visits them every day and night, and occasionally devours one of them for a meal." They were not satisfied to jog along rough roads at less than five miles an hour. They demanded better highways, lighter vehicles, and faster horses. Even the pulpit caught the spirit of the times.

On Thanksgiving Day, 1846, Dr. Horace Bushnell, one of the greatest of the nineteenth century New England Congregational ministers, preached a sermon entitled "Roads," in which he said: "If you wish to know whether society is stagnant, learning scholastic, religion a dead formality, you may learn something by going into universities and libraries; something also by the work that is doing on cathedrals and churches, or in them; but quite as much by looking at the roads. For if there is any motion in society, the road, which is the symbol of motion, will indicate the fact. When there is activity or enlargement or a liberalizing spirit of any kind, then there is intercourse and travel, and these require roads. So if there is any kind of advancement going on, if new ideas are abroad and new hopes rising, then you will see it by the roads that are building. Nothing makes an inroad without making a road. All creative action, whether in government, industry, thought, or religion, creates roads."

Sunday in Dr. Bushnell's time was not a very lively day on the roads. As a Rhode Island poet wrote:

> On Sabbath days the horse is seen
> Unshackled on the meadow green.

Horse cars were not permitted to run on the Lord's Day in Connecticut during the first years of the horse railways. But in September, 1870, the horse railway company of Norwich brightened the gloom by boldly defying the law and putting on Sunday cars, commencing at 9 A. M. and making hourly trips until 6 P. M. This was said to be for the accommodation of churchgoers. Bridgeport had started the innovation the year before, but did it by a technicality. The old Sunday law prohibited all work on Sunday except works of charity and mercy. To forestall anyone having the law enforced against the railroad company, a petition was circulated requesting the railway officials to put on Sunday cars so that works of charity and mercy could be performed. The directors of the company then adopted a vote establishing Sunday cars, representations having been made to them "that acts of charity and mercy would be advanced thereby."

Decent roads came slowly. The railroads—the steam-powered railroads, not the horsed railroads—killed off the main stage lines, but many local stages continued in operation all through the horse and buggy age, not even the coming of the trolley, which linked together scores of New England towns, entirely doing away with the need for them. A great number of places had neither steam nor electric connections with the outside world, though the mechanical means of transport were in no case very far away, and as the world shrank, people's backgrounds broadened. It was thought that the faster a man could travel, the more civilized he was, a notion that has persisted down to the present day.

But lately people have begun to view some of the results of rapid transport with disillusionment and to question the idea that because we can travel ten or a dozen times faster than our grandparents we are necessarily that much more civilized. All sorts of people are trying to escape from the complications of life in a mechanical age. They sigh for the simpler and slower days, the blessed Eden of the horse and buggy age.

Without attempting to strike a balance of profits and losses, it can be truthfully said that it was a grand epoch in which New England played a leading part.

THE CARRIAGE TRADE

CHAPTER II

The Carriage Trade

NEWPORT in the season was the place *par excellence*
for smart horses and carriages. Henry James in *An
International Episode* has described the town in the
Seventies, mentioning particularly the basket-phaetons
drawn by ponies, in which ladies of high fashion went
shopping. He speaks of the great number of these
basket-phaetons drawn up before the shops, or bump-
ing about on the cobblestones, the ladies greeting each
other from vehicle to vehicle and conversing on the
edge of the pavement, with a great many "Oh, my
dears," and little, quick exclamations and caresses.
Tripping in and out of their vehicles they displayed
nothing more than remarkably pretty feet, for which
they could hardly find a place in their phaetons when
they had finished shopping, so many bundles did they
accumulate at the bottoms of their carriages. Later,
about 1890, the delight of the feminine heart at both
Newport and Bar Harbor was the light, springy, little
buckboard of polished bird's-eye maple.

Henry James speaks of the famous Newport hotel, the Ocean House, which survived until the present century, but was not rebuilt after it burned. It was an enormous wooden structure, for the erection of which it seemed to him that the virgin forests of the West must have been terribly deflowered. "In front was a gigantic veranda, upon which an army might have encamped—a vast wooden terrace, with a roof as lofty as the nave of a cathedral." From this veranda on Sunday mornings in the days of corsets and button shoes one had an excellent view of the church parade—the high-stepping, satiny horses in shining harness, the men on the boxes of the victorias in white breeches and pink-topped or mahogany-topped boots, the ladies holding small carriage parasols and looking for all the world like the Continental drawings of Mr. Constantine Guys.

The best time, however, to see the spectacle of Newport was not on Sunday morning but late in the afternoon of a weekday. "On every fine day," wrote Samuel Adams Drake in 1876, "between four in the afternoon and dusk Bellevue Avenue is thronged with equipages, equestrians, and promenaders. Nowhere in America can so many elegant turnouts be seen as here; every specie of vehicle known to the wheeled vocabulary is in requisition. The cortége is not, as might be supposed, a racing mob, but a decorous-paced, well-reigned procession—a sort of reunion on wheels of all that is brilliant and fascinating in Newport society. The quiet though elegant carriages with crests on them are Bos-

tonian; the most stylish horse-furniture and mettled
horses are at home in Central Park; Philadelphia is
self-contained, and of substantial elegance. Imagine
this pageant of beautiful women and cultivated men
passing and repassing, mingling and separating, smil-
ing, saluting, admiring, and admired; the steady beat

THE DRIVE, NEWPORT

of hoofs on the hard gravel and continuous roll of
wheels proceeding without intermission, until the whole
becomes bewildering, confused, and indistinct, as if the
whirl of wheels were indeed in your brain."

A sensation was caused in the Eighties when one day
Mrs. August Belmont drove from the gates of her resi-
dence down Bellevue Avenue in a rig worthy of royalty.
To a handsome open phaeton were harnessed four
horses instead of the usual two horses. Postilions were
mounted on the backs of the off-wheeler and the
wheeler. They were dressed in white buckskin breeches,
short tailless coats of melton, and in place of the con-

ventional stovepipe a round visored hat resembling those worn by jockeys. Mrs. Belmont used to drive in state around Newport perhaps half a dozen times a season.

Toward the end of August many people migrated from the sea to the Berkshires, where Lenox was the fashionable center. It was the favorite place of Fanny Kemble, the actress, who owned a span of spirited black horses, behind which she enjoyed a spin over the country roads. She rode or drove to the summit of every notable mountain for twenty miles round Lenox.

For many years the styles in American vehicles were set by James Brewster, a pioneer carriage builder of New Haven, Connecticut. Brewster carriages and wagons were famous. They were looked on as the last word in construction and design. Brewster, who was born in Preston, Connecticut, learned the wagon-building trade in Northampton, Massachusetts, under the tutelage of Charles Chapman. When he was twenty-one he left for New York, but on reaching New Haven paid a casual visit to a carriage shop which he accidentally came across, and on being offered a job took off his coat and went to work. This was in 1810. The following year he opened his own shop in New Haven. The carriage trade was then in its infancy, but the building of turnpikes and the improvement in roads generally was beginning to create a large demand for light pleasure vehicles. Brewster concentrated on finely made carriages, his aim being to beat the English coach-builders. His productions soon became well known. In

1827 he opened a carriage repository and repair shop in New York.

Foreseeing the coming of the railroads, he devoted himself to the promotion and construction of a line between New Haven and Hartford and became the first president of the road. It was thought at the time that the railroads would cause a decline in the carriage trade, but the new wealth which the railroads brought to communities had exactly the opposite effect, stimulating rather than depressing the industry. After four years of railroad-building, Brewster went back to carriage-building, manufacturing many different kinds in a variety of models—buggies, phaetons, carryalls, coaches, victorias, and numerous other styles. He did not allow his workmen to use liquor. He became rich, and during the Civil War equipped a whole regiment at his own expense. His benefactions to New Haven were numerous. He died in 1866, but his name stood for many years as a hallmark of soundly-designed carriages.

A year or two after James Brewster set himself up as a carriage-builder in New Haven another young man opened a carriage shop in Concord, New Hampshire, which was to send the name of that town rolling round the world. Concord wagons and coaches became known everywhere. By reason of the materials and workmanship which went to their making they could stand an extraordinary amount of hard usage. The coaches in particular, which were designed and constructed for travel over our unimproved or partly improved American roads, could be used under conditions which would have speedily put an English coach out of commission. For this reason they were preferred even in Australia and South Africa to coaches of British manufacture. The opening and development of new countries and territories during the nineteenth century kept the New Hampshire coach-builders busy all through the horse and buggy years.

The youthful initiator of the carriage industry in Concord was Lewis Downing. In an advertisement in the *New Hampshire Patriot* of August 3, 1813, he respectfully informed the inhabitants of Concord and vicinity that he had commenced the wheelwright business in Concord. Born in Lexington, Massachusetts, June 23, 1792, he learned the carriage building trade from his father and brother, both of whom were said to have been skilled workers. His capital consisted of his tools and sixty dollars in cash.

In November, 1813, the first Concord wagon was sold by Downing to Benjamin Kimball, Jr., for sixty dollars.

During Downing's first year in business he worked alone, doing everything by hand and using no power machinery whatever, which shows that he must have been a versatile workman. After the first year he employed from three to six hands. This continued for about a dozen years, when he enlarged his shop and started all the different branches connected with the carriage trade—blacksmithing, painting, trimming, etc.—and employed from thirty to forty men. Besides Concord wagons, he made a heavier type of transport wagon for the newly inaugurated freight service be-

tween Boston and points in New Hampshire and Vermont, and also chaises. In 1826 he decided to go in for
coach-building. From Salem he got a young workman
named J. Stephens Abbot to come to Concord and make
three coach bodies, the balance of the work being done
by Downing.

The result of this collaboration, the first Concord

CONCORD WAGON

coach, was sold to a stage-driver, John Shepard, in
July, 1827.

The next year we find Downing taking young Abbot
into partnership. They worked together in double
harness until 1847, when the partnership was dissolved.
Abbot kept the old carriage shop and took his oldest
son into business, the new firm doing business under the
name of J. S. and E. A. Abbot. Downing built a new
shop and took his two sons, Lewis, Jr., and Alonzo, in
with him.

In 1855 both Downing and Abbot made statements
concerning their respective businesses. Downing said:

"Since 1847 I have employed from forty to seventy hands; now seventy hands, and could sell the work of twice that number, but my practice has ever been to do no more business than I could see to personally." Abbot said: "In 1854 we sent carriages into every State, Territory, and Province in North America (except Delaware); also Mexico and South America. We

BROUGHAM

employed averaging one hundred and ninety men; delivered six hundred and twenty-five carriages, and used 300,000 feet of lumber, fifty tons of Cumberland coal, 6500 bushels of charcoal. We cannot now name the exact amount of iron, but about two hundred and fifty tons."

During the Civil War both firms had all the work they could do making gun carriages, ambulances, and quartermasters' wagons for the government.

Lewis Downing, Sr., retired January 1, 1865, and the two firms were merged into Abbot, Downing and Company. In 1873 the business was incorporated, becoming the Abbot-Downing Company, which absorbed another Concord carriage house, Harvey, Morgan and Company. Two hundred and seventy-five men were employed in the shops, which covered six acres. There were also several other carriage manufacturers in Concord, each employing from sixty to a hundred hands.

The Concord coach as developed by the Downings and the Abbots was made of wood and designed to hold

PANEL BOOT VICTORIA

nine passengers, three on a seat. The center seat was nothing but a bench made in three sections, the ends of which turned up to give access to the front and rear seats. There was no back to this middle seat. The passengers were supported by a broad leather strap held in place by other straps suspended from the roof of the coach and fastened below. No springs were used in the Concord coaches. The bodies were hung on leather thorough-braces and naturally swayed when the vehicles were running. The backward and forward motion of the coaches made some people ill. The driver had to be careful to meet this motion with his arms so as not to pull on the horses.

The materials and workmanship used in making a

coach had to be of the best. The wood for the body, which was four feet six inches in width, was the toughest ash taken from exposed situations and seasoned for at least two years. Equally carefully selected oak, hickory, and elm were used in other parts of the coach. Spanish cedar was often used for the panels, with some ornamental work in mahogany or rosewood. The coach body was a piece of the finest joiner's work. The greatest care was also taken with the frame and axles, in which there was a good deal of metal work. The wheels were the most important part of the coach. To give the greatest strength with the least possible weight, three kinds of wood were used—elm for the nave, oak for the spokes, and ash for the felloes. A great improvement was brought about in the Eighteen-thirties, when an American blacksmith decided that instead of making the tire in separate plates and attaching them to the wheel over the joints of the felloes, he would make the tire in one piece and drive it on while hot, thus taking advantage of the binding power of the cooling and contracting metal. This American invention added greatly to the strength of the wheels. The hind wheels of the Concord coaches measured five feet one inch in diameter, the front wheels three feet ten inches. A Concord coach weighing 2400 pounds sold for $2400.

A curious custom which survived from the early days of stage-coaching down into the era of fashionable road-coaching was that a coach did not carry its lamps during the day time. Apparently the reason for this was that in the old stage-coach days the stage-driver left the coach lamps to be filled at the first place the horses were changed after dawn and the stage coaches were therefore always without lamps during the day runs.

Amesbury, Massachusetts, was another important New England carriage trade center. Statistics of the carriage trade there for the year 1880 show that twenty-five concerns produced over 12,000 carriages and sleighs worth more than a million dollars. Approximately eight hundred highly-skilled men—designers, body-makers, wheelwrights, metal workers, carvers, upholsterers, painters, etc.—were employed in the carriage shops there. The oldest and largest shop in Amesbury at that time was R. F. Briggs and Company, which was founded in 1856. The one hundred and twenty-five men employed in this shop turned out 1800 vehicles annually.

But the carriage shops of Amesbury, Concord, and New Haven were not the only ones in New England. There were small shops everywhere. From these small shops came many inventions and improvements of importance to the carriage trade. Benjamin Lyman, for example, who had a wagon shop in Manchester, Connecticut, was the inventor of the iron hub used in carts and drays. When iron hubs were not used, black locust was the wood favored for the hubs of vehicles of the heavier type. It was kept on hand in various sizes and after the bark had been stripped off was bored to facilitate seasoning. All wood used in wagon and carriage building was seasoned one year for every inch of thickness, which necessitated the outlay of considerable capital to keep a supply on hand, since it required three or four or more years to season some of the wood used in the trade. Our native woods gave us a great natural advantage in carriage construction. This advantage in raw materials, coupled with the work of our mechanics, placed the country in the forefront as a manufacturer of all kinds of carriages. Not only those which were adoptions from and improvements on foreign models, but those which we originated ourselves and were characteristically American. Our vehicles were distinguished by their lightness, strength, durability, and comfort. Our wheels were unbeatable. Before the close of the horse and buggy age most of the world was rolling around on American-made wheels.

At first entire vehicles were built in the small shops, but with the increased demand for carriages, factories began turning out parts, such as wheels, axles, top frames, springs, etc., of every pattern, and the small carriage-builder became chiefly an assembler. Then there was the local distributor for the large carriage manufacturers who kept a stock of new and second-hand vehicles and did repairing and painting. It took a great deal of space to store carriages, and many people will remember the small town carriage shops and repositories with their long runways for getting the carriages above the ground floor. In Stamford, Connecticut, a Congregational church was converted into a carriage shop.

The first carriage-builders to apply mass production methods in their shops were Messrs. G. and D. Cook of New Haven, who in the late Fifties began systematizing the work in their shops. They stepped up their production from one carriage a day to ten, or at the rate of one an hour. People marveled at the facility with which they could turn them out. They employed three hundred men in the twenty-four departments of their business. The assembly line of the modern motor-car plant may, I think, be said to have had its origin in this Connecticut carriage shop.

But with carriages as with other things, the ready-made, mass-produced article did not do away with the custom-made product. Here and there in New England were carriage shops that specialized in building vehicles to order. There was no city of any size that did not have its fashionable carriage-maker who could build anything in the way of a vehicle, from a racing sulky—the name, by the way, is derived from the fact that the driver wishes to be alone—to a Russian droshky. An advertisement of one of these carriage-builders mentions the following vehicles as among those he stood ready to make to order:

Barouches,	Landaulets,
Broughams,	Landaus,
Cabriolets,	Light Rockaways,
Coaches,	One-Man Wagons,
Coupe Rockaways,	Canopy-Top Phaetons,
Coupes,	Physicians' Phaetons,
Depot Wagons,	Pony Phaetons,
Dog Carts,	Road Wagons,
Buggies,	Rockaways,
Ladies' Phaetons,	Rockelets,

Rumble Phaetons,	Village Carts,
Skeleton Wagons,	Vis-a-Vis,
Sulkies,	Victorias,
Surreys,	Wagonettes,
T Carts,	Extention-Top Phaetons.

Among the vehicles that were characteristically American were the buggy, the carryall, the surrey, the rockaway, the station wagon, and their derivatives. At first the condition of our roads permitted the use of only the strongest and lightest types of English and Continental carriages, and of these the two-wheeled French chaise was the most popular. It was the forerunner of the buggy, and as developed in this country, with its leather thorough-braces, hickory shafts, and adjustable hood, was a comfortable and roomy all-weather vehicle. Although the buggy came into general use in the Fifties, it did not entirely displace the two-wheel chaise until after the Civil War. The buggy, of which the carryall was really a two-seated version, was evolved as a result of better road building and maintenance. It was the outgrowth of a need for a four-wheel conveyance which would be easier on the horse than the two-wheeler and at the same time would preserve the comfort of the chaise. It was really the body of the chaise on a four-wheel under carriage. It was about 1835 that the buggy took the general form that was characteristic of it during the horse and buggy age. Improvements in carriage construction brought about changes in it, and there were, of course, many different styles and models, but on the whole no better vehicle for riding comfort and ease of driving was ever devised for two passengers.

Most of the fine upholstery cloths, nets, damasks, plushes, and coach laces used in the carriage trade were made in the textile mills of New England.

HARNESS-MAKERS AND SADDLERS

CHAPTER III

Harness-Makers and Saddlers

A PLEASANT smell of leather and beeswax was the first thing I noticed when I entered the historic harness house of the Smith-Worthington Saddlery Company in Hartford, Connecticut. The plant, a dim old brick affair with multi-paned windows, stands on the brink of the Hog River, not far from the spot where Colonel Albert Pope made Columbia bicycles and Pope-Hartford automobiles. Its spacious old-fashioned showroom contains a great array of saddles, bridles, bits, blankets, harness, and all kinds of horse gear, and an extensive variety of riding and driving sundries. For me the place reversed the wheel of time to bring back the horse and buggy age. Here was the old New England harness shop once more. But there was one thing missing. I remembered the stuffed horse, or perhaps it was a plaster or wooden horse, used as a dummy to display harness, which stood for years in the firm's downtown

31

shop. The shop was moved to the plant long ago, but I had hoped to find the dapple gray had survived. I wanted to see it again, but it was nowhere to be seen. I concluded that it must have been given to a cigar store Indian in search of a mount.

As I glanced about the showroom I began to wish the person I had come to see would keep me waiting a long time, so that I could look at everything, but in a moment I was greeted by Mr. Roberts, the present head of the concern, who has been connected with the company for nearly half a century, though to look at him—alert and active—you would hardly believe this to be the case. I had come to see him by appointment and he knew I wanted information about his business.

"What became of the wooden horse which used to stand in your Asylum Street shop?" I asked.

Mr. Roberts smiled. "One of its legs got broken," he said, "and we had to shoot it."

"I have heard that this is the largest harness shop in the country."

"It's the largest in the world," said Mr. Roberts modestly. "We have made harness here for everything except fleas. We have made it for goats and we have made it for burros. We have made it for elephants and we have made it for zebras. We have made pack harness for the llamas in the Andes and dog harness for Polar expeditions. Right now we are making a lot of dog harness. There isn't a place in the world, from Australia to the Mountains of the Moon, where our goods haven't been used. But won't you step into the office?" he said. "We can sit down in there."

And seated beside a table on which were a number of horse magazines Mr. Roberts gave me what I came for—a sketch of the history of his business.

It was on August 9, 1794, that a Connecticut Yankee named Normand Smith opened a saddlery and harness shop at the Sign of the Mounted Dragoon on the north corner of Main and Temple Streets in Hartford. The provincial capital or semi-capital—at that time Hartford shared the governmental honor equally with New Haven—was a town of between four and five thousand inhabitants, with about forty shops, mostly in the houses of the shopkeepers, a number of merchants, and a strong smell of molasses and Jamaica rum. It was the head of sloop navigation on the Connecticut, River and enjoyed a thriving trade not only with the West Indies but by means of flat-bottomed boats with the up-river towns as far north as Wells River, Vermont. It was, moreover, a trading center for a great many towns not on the river, to which goods were freighted in wagons. It was, in short, a promising place for Normand Smith to open a harness shop.

But the results must have exceeded his greatest expectations. The enterprise prospered until it became the country's leading saddlery and harness business. It made Hartford the center of the harness trade during the golden years of the horse. For one hundred and eleven years the business was carried on by only two generations of partners—Normand Smith and his two sons. Today, after nearly a century and a half of activity, it is still being carried on by the business associates of the sons of the founder. Some of the men employed by the Smith-Worthington Saddlery Company first went to work there in the horse and buggy era.

In 1818 the firm established a branch in New Orleans, where a large stock of horse goods from Hartford was kept on hand for the Southern trade. Later another branch was opened at Louisville. Shipments were made to New Orleans by coastwise vessels. In winter when the Connecticut River was closed to navigation and New Haven harbor was frozen over, leather merchandise was sent overland to New York and shipped south in sailing packets. It was not unusual for shipments to be made all the way from Hartford to St. Louis by water, the goods upon arrival being paid for in buffalo skins at nine dollars a bale.

Preserved in the old letter-book of the firm, which Mr. Roberts showed me, are many interesting missives relating to the shipment and payment of goods. One letter ordering short-haired horse hides suitable for making into trunks, to be shipped from New York to Hartford on the sloop *Burdette*, urges all possible speed in the execution of the order, since it was then the twenty-second of November and it was feared that at any moment the river would freeze and be closed to commerce until spring. Freight rates were much higher for transporting goods in wagons.

Another letter accompanying a parcel of notes and bills of exchange sent in payment of material supplied to the Hartford concern lists the notes and other commercial paper in detail and states that these negotiable instruments have been cut in two and only half of each

note forwarded with the letter, the corresponding halves
being held for a later stage-coach as a measure of
protection against loss by robbery.

But more interesting than the letter-book, with its
clear, bold handwriting, in a full, little leather bound
volume, a hand-made catalogue used in connection with
the firm's Southern trade, in which are miniature water-
color pictures drawn to scale and beautifully colored,
showing all the different types of saddles made by the
company. As I looked through the book, I was reminded
of nothing so much as an illuminated manuscript of the
time before printing. Larger paintings in antique wal-
nut frames, also of saddles, adorn the walls of the
Smith-Worthington office. Some of the saddles pictured
are of patterns never used in this country, but which
at one time or another were made expressly for exporting to foreign countries.

The exporting end of the business made it necessary
for the firm to have a branch in New York, and accordingly one was opened in 1842 at the Sign of the
Golden Saddle, No. 10 Old Slip. Through this branch
for many years was handled the importation of thousands of English saddle-trees used in making the better
class riding-saddles. These saddle-trees are mostly of
English beech, a light-weight, close-fibered, long-lived
wood, which is springy and does not check easily. This
last feature is an important one, because in saddle-
making the saddler drives from five hundred to seven
hundred tacks into the saddle-tree.

The Civil War ruined the firm's Southern business,
but this was more than compensated for at the time by

government orders for military equipment. Six hundred people were employed in this war work. Other wars have likewise meant a rush of business, the World War bringing a great spate of orders. One order from the Russian government was for 10,000 saddles. In five months the Smith-Worthington Saddlery Company produced 25,000 saddles, a figure that becomes impressive immediately it is remembered that very little machinery is used in making saddles.

"Does the government buy harness and saddlery from you now?" I asked Mr. Roberts.

"It supplies all its own peacetime needs," he answered. "It's the largest cutter of leather in the country. The work's done at the Jeffersonville Arsenal."

"I am curious about russet harness. Was there really a great deal made in the old days?"

"Not such an awful lot," he said. "It was called advertising harness and was used mostly for show. We had a couple of trucks in New York with russet harness for the horses. But it didn't last. It turned black in six months. Russet reins were popular, though."

"Is there any demand now for four-in-hand harness?"

Mr. Roberts shook his head. "About a year ago we had an order for a set from the Pacific coast. From Oregon, I think. I told one of our old harness-makers about it. He thought I was joking until I showed him the order. 'There it is,' I said. 'Go ahead and make it.'"

"Those big fancy buttons used to decorate bridles, which antique shops now sell for curtain tie-backs—are they scarce? I have some with American eagles and flags in color. They're brassbound buttons, two or three inches across, with the pictures under glass."

"Rosettes," said Mr. Roberts. "They still make them even in Pawtucket. The commonest were those with horses' heads."

"Where does most of the harness hardware come from?"

"New Britain. They've been making harness buckles in New Britain for a hundred years. They make stirrups, too."

"How many patterns of saddles does Smith-Worthington turn out nowadays, Mr. Roberts?"

"H'mm," he said, making a mental calculation, and then at length, "fifty."

"And more people than ever are riding horseback today?"

"More than at any time in our history."

His secretary interrupted to say that one of the company's travelers was on the long distance wire about an order for a Greenwich stable and wanted to speak to Mr. Roberts. He took the call and then turned back to me.

"Do you see that jockey saddle?" he said.

I turned my head.

"How much do you think it weighs?" he asked.

I shook my head.

"Complete with furniture," said Mr. Roberts, "it weighs just thirty-two ounces."

"Do you make many side-saddles?" I inquired.

"A few. Women who learned to ride that way in days

gone by still use them. They're used some in horse shows. But they're a thing of the past."

At one time a number of different firms were engaged in the saddlery business in Bridgeport, Connecticut, but none, apparently, on so extensive a scale as the Smith-Worthington Saddlery Company of Hartford.

Another New England harness center was Springfield, Massachusetts, where W. H. Wilkinson amassed a fortune manufacturing harness and saddlery. During the Civil War he supplied the government with $1,500,-000 worth of harness and saddles. The transport and commissariat teams of the first ten regiments that went to the war from Connecticut were equipped by him, and he made for the government the model artillery harness, complete sets of which were presented to the Italian and Swiss governments. While engaged in this government work he employed about four hundred hands. Normally the number was around one hundred. A former partner of his, Josiah Cummings, was also largely engaged during the rebellion on government contracts in Springfield. He employed from three to four hundred hands and supplied the government with a million dollars' worth of military equipment. After the war his trade extended all through the United States and his harnesses were bought "by the most wealthy gentlemen in the large cities." Like most of the harness-makers and saddlers of the time, Josiah Cummings was also a trunk-maker. He made leather trunks and valises of all kinds.

Concord, New Hampshire, famous for its wagons, carriages, and coaches, was also noted for the harness that was made there. This business was started when James R. Hill began making harness in Concord in the Eighteen-forties. In 1865 he took George H. Emery and Josiah E. Dwight into partnership, and it was this firm that made the reputation of the town for harness. Upward of a hundred men were employed, some of them French-Canadians. The fine quality of the leather used and the skillful workmanship made Concord harnesses almost as well known as Concord vehicles.

As for the small retail harness shops, which once flourished everywhere but are now extinct, no better idea of them can be conveyed than by quoting from an advertisement of one in which is given a list of the stock in trade it carried. The advertisement is from a New England city directory for the year 1860.

Harnesses, Trunks, Saddles & Collars.
Our Stock Consists of the Following Goods.

HARNESS.
Buggy, Phaeton, Tandam, Trotting, Droskie, Coach, Hack, Draft.

TRUNKS.
Sole Leather, Ladies' Dress, Ladies' Hat, Ladies' French, Single, Double, Folio and Valises.

SADDLES.
Ladies' Quilted, Ladies' Plain, Gents' Somerset, Gents' Plain, Boys' Pilchs, Girls' Pilchs, English Saddles, Mexican Saddles.

WHIPS.

Buggy, Phaeton, Hack, Ladies' and Gents' Riding Whips.

BITS.

Pelham, Buxton, Single Snaffles, Double Snaffles, Arch and Port, Military, Embossed, Steel Curb.

HORSE CLOTHING.

Summer, various patterns, Winter, various patterns, Knee Caps, Ear Nets, Neck, Flank and Body Nets, Rollers, Surcingles.

Also Brushes, Combs and Curry Combs.

Russet Round and Flat Riding and Driving Bridles.

Fancy Leather Riding Bridles, Plated Martingales.

Hand Pieces, Holders, Buttons, Children's Chaises, Dusters, Mats.

Pole Straps, Rubber Clothing, Sleigh Bells, Halters.

COLLARS and INTERFERING BOOTS made to fit the most difficult leg or neck. REPAIRING, OILING, &c.

No Stitching Machines used in this Establishment.

The last line is significant. Most of the small harness shops did not have sewing machines, which cost about $650 apiece, and the harness-makers appealed to the prejudices of people in favor of hand work by advertising that no machine stitching was done in their

shops. Custom-made harness was a hand job anyway
and so was most repair work. Mending harness was a
major part of the business of the small harness shops.
One of these shops which I remember was a small
bow-windowed place which stood next door to a wood
engraver's and had the following admonition across its
front in gilt letters: "A Stitch in Time Saves Nine."
It was a very apt slogan for a harness-maker. Cheap,
ready-made harness, costing, say, from thirteen to
seventeen dollars for a single set and proportionately
more for a double set, needed constant attention. It was
poor economy to buy it. It did not last and was sometimes the cause of accidents. I was a witness to a runaway caused by defective harness. A grocery team was
going down a hill, when suddenly the backstrap broke,
the wagon ran against the horse's legs, and the animal
bolted, smashing the wagon and injuring itself. When
it came to buying harness, the best was none too good.

A fine set of custom-made single harness could be
had for fifty dollars and a set of double harness for
one hundred and fifty dollars. This included silver
mountings instead of brass, with your initial or mono-
gram on the blinkers. There were as many conventions
and niceties of detail to be observed in harnessing horses
correctly as there were in matters of personal dress.
The proper shape for the blinkers, for example, on a
set of driving harness was square or with only slightly
rounded corners. D-shaped, horseshoe shaped, and
round blinkers were usually seen only on cab, grocery,
and cart horses. Similarly, buckles were also square or
slightly rounded on the edge, save in the case of harness

used for sporting purposes, when horseshoe-shaped buckles were permissible. In sporting outfits the collars might be faced with tan leather, otherwise the proper facing was black. And the pattern of the harness depended on the kind of vehicle with which it was to be used. A heavy harness designed for drawing a brougham was not the thing to use with a light carriage.

The wise owner put the cart before both the horse and the harness. He decided first what kind of a carriage he would keep, bought the right size and kind of horse to go with it, and then ordered harness that was appropriate for both horse and carriage. The man who threw himself on the mercies of a first-rate harness-maker pursued the wisest course.

YANKEE BLACKSMITHS

CHAPTER IV

Yankee Blacksmiths

THE spreading chestnut-tree under which stood the village smithy of Longfellow's celebrated poem, *The Village Blacksmith,* was chopped down in 1876. It over-hung a blacksmith's shop near the poet's house in Cambridge. When Longfellow heard that the authorities planned to remove the aged horse-chestnut-tree, he and others protested. But American local government officials seem to have inherited from the father of our country a propensity for cutting down trees, and all pleas to spare it failed. The excuse given for destroying the tree was that it was a menace to those driving under it with heavy loads.

Undoubtedly the outstanding blacksmith in New England in the horse and buggy days was Elihu Burritt of New Britain, Connecticut. He became widely known in this country and Europe as The Learned Blacksmith. The youngest of ten children, he was born

in the year 1810 in New Britain, where there is now a
hotel and a school named after him. At the age of sixteen he was obliged to leave school and was apprenticed
to a blacksmith. But leaving school to learn a trade did
not quench his thirst for knowledge. All his spare time
was spent in study. Sometimes he snatched a few minutes at the anvil to pore over a diminutive Greek
grammar which he carried about in his hat or pocket.
He learned Greek and Hebrew so he could read the
Bible in the original. By the time he was twenty-one
he had acquired a knowledge not only of the classical
languages, but also French, German, Italian, and
Spanish. He spent a winter in New Haven because of
the library facilities there and the presence of scholars.
Then for a year he was preceptor in an academy where
he taught languages. But he overworked and had to
give up teaching. He became a traveler for a New
Britain manufacturer and then opened a grocery store
in his native town. In the panic of 1837 he lost everything and decided to take up his trade and his studies
again. This he did in Worcester, Massachusetts, where
he took full advantage of the rich storehouse of books
in the library of the Antiquarian Society.

Burritt had a reforming spirit and the zeal of a
missionary. From Worcester he began going about the
country giving lectures when he was not too busy shoeing horses. The fact that he was a blacksmith who had
taught himself to speak fifty languages, most of which
the people to whom he lectured had probably never even
heard of, doubtless made him something of a freak attraction at first. But his idealism and honesty and the

earnest crusading way in which he hammered his Yankee notions into his audiences won him many friends and spread his fame. His was no Panglossian theory of life. Not everything was for the best in this best possible of worlds. He saw the evil that men do and understood their misunderstanding of each other. He wished to win all men to a wider vision and a deeper sympathy, to guide their footsteps in the ways of honor, freedom, fellowship, and peace. The self-taught blacksmith became famous as an advocate of world concord.

In 1848 he hung up his leather apron and went to England on a lecture tour. He intended to stay only three months, but remained three years. He drew crowded houses in both England and Ireland. He was in Ireland during the terrible famine of 1846-7. In 1848 he was vice-president of the Peace Congress held in Brussels, and was secretary of the Paris Peace Congress of 1849. He attended the Exeter Hall meetings in London in 1849 and 1851, and the one in Frankfort in 1850. He organized the friends of peace at Brussels, Paris, Frankfort, London, Manchester, and Edinburgh, this work for the League of Universal Brotherhood bringing him into close touch with many distinguished men, including John Bright, Richard Cobden, Victor Hugo, Alexis de Tocqueville, and Alexander von Humboldt, whom he counted as his friends.

The Learned Blacksmith returned to America in 1850 for a lecture tour. Again, after the Edinburgh Peace Congress of 1853, he was here advocating ocean penny postage. He made speeches and spent some time in Washington lobbying for the measure. The next

year he re-visited England in the interests of the peace
movement. On his return to this country he threw himself into the Abolitionist cause, lecturing on Compensated Emancipation. He was for peace at almost any
price and became secretary of the organization formed
in 1856 to promote this scheme. After some years spent
on his farm in New Britain, he went to England again
in 1863, this visit resulting in two books, *A Walk from
London to John O'Groat's* and *A Walk From London
to Land's End and Back*, both of which were published
in London. In 1865 he was made United States Con-
sular Agent at Birmingham, where, during his consul-
ship, he gathered material for still another book, *Walks
in the Black Country and Its Green Border Lands*.
This was followed by *The Mission of Great Sufferings*.
He was also an indefatigable pamphleteer. In 1870 he
returned to New Britain, establishing two mission
schools, one on his farm and the other in a chapel built
chiefly with his own hands. Elihu Burritt was in his
sixty-ninth year when he died in 1879.

Another Connecticut man, George J. Capewell of
Cheshire, who invented an automatic horse nail machine,
became the horse nail king of America. On his monument in Cedar Hill Cemetery in Hartford—he died in
1919—there are, fittingly enough, four beautifully
sculptured horseshoes, two on the front of the monument and two on the back, perfect in every detail, with
a large horse nail across each shoe. Before Mr. Capewell
came into the field with his machine, other machines for
making horse nails had been patented, notably one invented about 1848 by L. G. Reynolds of Providence,

the inventor of the solid-headed pin; but none of the earlier machines was so satisfactory or so successful as the Capewell machine. A company was organized to exploit the new machine, and the manufacture of horse nails was begun in rented quarters in Hartford in 1881. As the superiority of the Capewell nails was proved in active service, the business expanded rapidly, and under the management of the Williams family was developed into the largest horse nail business in the world. Aaron W. C. Williams, who had played an important part in the founding of the business and was one of its first officers, was joined by his nephew, Dr. G. C. F. Williams, who became the directing head of the company and managed it for over forty years. More than half of the horseshoe nails used in America during the great decades of the horse and buggy age were made by this Connecticut concern and its branch factory in Toronto.

The special virtue of the Capewell horse nails was that they did not crimp or split in driving into the hardest hoof and were flexible enough to twist and clinch, holding the clinch against any strain in service and never breaking under the heads. They held the shoe until it was worn out. They were uniform in length, breadth, and thickness, and were easy to drive, because from head to point they had a highly polished finish that reduced friction to a minimum. They were made from the best Swedish steel rods, practically free from chemical impurities, the quality of which was further improved in increased compactness, tenacity, and uniformity of temper, under the Capewell process of cold rolling its product. By reducing the blade from the cold stock a nail was produced that was stronger than the original material from which it was made. Drawn from head to point, the nails had a tensile strength one half greater than those made by any other process.

Blacksmiths everywhere recognized the superiority of these nails. Fifty foreign countries were supplied with them. This export market was established and developed when the domestic demand began to fall off before the advance of the automobile. Different countries use different types or styles of horse nails, and to meet the demands of its foreign customers the Capewell Company found itself manufacturing more than four hundred different varieties of horse nails.

In 1936 Dr. Williams' son, Mr. Staunton Williams, the present head of the concern, brought about the merger with his company of the Fowler and Union Horse Nail Company, a Connecticut corporation, which owned and operated a factory in Buffalo, New York, and was the successor of the Chicago Horse Nail Company, the Northwestern Horse Nail Company, the Union Horse Nail Company, and the Fowler Nail Company. Although the word "horse" was dropped from the name of the new corporation, which became simply the Capewell Manufacturing Company, it continues to supply the world with horseshoe nails and still quotes in its advertisements the familiar lines of that old Bostonian, Benjamin Franklin:

> For the want of a nail the shoe was lost,
> For the want of a shoe the horse was lost,

For the want of a horse the rider was lost,
For the want of a rider the battle was lost,
For the want of a battle the kingdom was lost—
All for the want of a horseshoe nail.

Many a schoolboy fight in the horse and buggy days
was won by the boy whose fingers were covered with
rings made of horseshoe nails. One never sees these rings
any more, but of course there are no longer friendly
blacksmiths to give horse nails to boys who visit their
forges or even make the rings for them. Worn with the
heads out, a set of horse nail rings was as deadly as
a pair of knuckle-dusters.

A boy whose father was a blacksmith in Hartford,
and whose first riding is said to have been done delivering customers' horses from his father's smithy, became
one of the greatest jockeys America has produced. This
was Danny Maher, thrice winner of the English Derby.
Not only was this New England boy the champion
jockey of his time, but he was also one of the most
popular persons that ever climbed into a saddle. He
won more than fourteen hundred races in America and
abroad, including, in addition to the Epsom event,
many other turf classics, particularly in England,
where he did most of his racing. The Oaks, the Ascot
Gold Cup, the Doncaster St. Leger, the Two Thousand
Guineas, and the Sandown Eclipse Stakes were among
his triumphs. In his great days he rode over a hundred
winners in a single season of flat racing.

Danny took his first mount when he was only thirteen
years old, in a race at Providence in 1895. Three years

later he astonished the oldest racing men in the country
when he beat the record for a day's winning mounts
by bringing five horses under the wire first at the
Brighton Beach track. He won the Brooklyn Handicap
and bounded into the front rank of American race
riders. Danny was not trained, as is sometimes stated,
in the hard school of Father Bill Daly of Hartford, the
famous maker of jockeys, but by Father Bill Daly's
brother, Mike Daly, the race horse trainer, who married
Danny's aunt. Mike Daly took Danny in hand before
he reached his teens.

"The first time he put me on a horse was in 1891,"
said Danny, "when he was bringing some horses down
Fifth Avenue, en route to the Merchantville track. I
was nine years of age and weighed thirty-two pounds.
A great throng of people followed us. It was a strange
sight to them to see such a midget on a race horse. In
a very short time he began to put me through the
stunts, and devised all sorts of bits and reins so arranged that I could control my horse. I was old enough
to understand, but not very strong. The Mike Daly
bit was the outgrowth of my frailty. He also invented
some reins that went from the bit ring down to the
cinch, on and over a pulley block, back to the bit ring
again, and from there up to my hands. When I wanted
to hold my horse in I simply pulled his head right down
and back and he had to stop. I could have stopped an
elephant with those reins.

" 'Dan,' said Uncle Mike to me, when I began, 'never
let go of a horse's head. Always keep the reins on him.
That is the most important thing of all, my boy. The

minute you release your absolute power over a horse he is likely to conduct things his own way and you cease to be his master.'

"He impressed upon me the necessity for riding with the knees bent up. The way he explained it was that if a man lit on his feet stiff-legged he would jar himself and also the floor, whereas if he bent his knees there would be a less jar. He made it very clear by saying that it might break a spring wagon to load it up with a ton of coal and then drive over a rut. The coal being almost dead weight would jolt the vehicle. But if the same vehicle went over the same rut with twenty-five hundred pounds of hay, it would not suffer at all, as the hay would give with the shock and exercise its elasticity. It's the same way with a jockey. He has got to have elasticity to save a horse.

"Uncle Mike put me on to all those things and taught me to hold my position in a race until it was time to get down to the finish. If I was behind in a start, and the horse ahead of me was likely to get to the half in 0:49, I would not try to get there with him, as it would perhaps be necessary for me to make the distance in 0:48. Then in the finish I would have to send my mount along in another struggle, and the two might perhaps be too much for the beast. But save it all up for the stretch and get the result of one good effort."

Shortly after he won his first classic, the Brooklyn Handicap, the whole course of Maher's career was changed by a charge of wrongdoing brought against him as the result of an unfortunate incident in the Suburban Handicap at Sheepshead Bay. In that race he had the mount on Banastar, the horse with which he had won the Brooklyn Handicap, and the owner, William H. Clarke, a Tammany politician and Corporation Counsel of New York, had backed the horse heavily to win the Suburban. The no-recall system of starting was not then in vogue. Banastar had moved off well in several false starts, but when the barrier was finally released, Banastar stopped to kick the horse beside him and was left at the post. Mr. Clarke, angered because Maher beat the horse severely in an effort to overtake the field, charged him with having pulled Banastar deliberately and demanded that his license be suspended. The stewards investigated, but found the charges of wrongdoing were not sustained.

Partly as a result of the Banastar episode and partly because Maher was having difficulty in making the weight requirements, he decided to go to England. John Meehan, the restaurant proprietor and race horse owner, had proved a friend to Danny Maher in his trouble. He knew Maher was honest and had helped him. He now persuaded Clarke to release him from his contract and let Andrew Jackson Joyner have him. Joyner was training a public stable. It was these two men who in 1900 sent Danny Maher to England.

At that time most of the English jockeys were trained to ride with the long stirrup, the American crouch, now universal, being then an innovation in England. It undoubtedly helped Danny Maher to win many races, though he was a wonderful judge of pace and of a finish and could get more out of a horse than any rider of his day. His first Derby victory came in

1903 when he was up on Sir James Miller's Rock Sand. In 1905 he won again, this time on Cicero, one of Lord Rosebery's horses. Lord Rosebery once said that his three ambitions in life were to be Prime Minister of England, to win the Derby, and to marry the richest woman in the realm; he realized all three of his ambitions. He paid Danny Maher a retainer of $20,000 a year for first call on his services, while Lord Derby paid him $10,000 annually for second call. But when Danny Maher won the Derby for the third time in 1906 his mount was Spearmint, whose owner was Major Eustace Loder—"Lucky Loder." It is estimated that during the thirteen years of Danny Maher's career as a jockey on the English turf he made more than a million dollars.

One thing he did with his money was to open a café on the Main Street of the New England city in which he was born. It was a splendidly appointed place, the bar alone costing $20,000. Its central feature was a life-size horse's head of mahogany, with a practical bit and bridle. On the opposite wall were pictures of Danny's Derby winners and other horses he rode to victory. One might suppose that being a jockey he would have fancied having a horseshoe bar, especially because he really built the place for his father and the former blacksmith managed it during his son's absence in England; but Maher's Café was long and narrow like a Pullman car and a straight bar was the only feasible kind for such a place.

Danny Maher retired from the turf in 1914 owing to ill health and died two years later in England. He was thirty-four years old. He was the idol of the English racing world and a great personal favorite of many of the leading men of England. He lies in Paddington Cemetery, London.

Whether or not Danny Maher learned anything about horseshoeing from his father, I do not know. The shoeing of horses, especially race horses, is an art, and it was many years before much was known about such matters as weight and balance. The gait of some early race horses might have been improved had the knowledge of later years been available in their day. All sorts of theories were held as to the proper way to shoe horses, and horsy people in this as in other matters were inclined to be rather intolerant of each other's opinions.

To find a good horseshoer was not always an easy thing to do. Many of the brawny-armed blacksmiths of the picturesque New England village smithies were incompetent. They butchered the horses' hoofs, cutting and burning them to fit the shoes, instead of fitting the shoes to the hoofs. But probably you would have welcomed even the unskilled services of one of these smiths on one of those Sunday afternoons in the horse and buggy age when you planned to go for a drive but could not because you discovered your horse had cast a shoe.

At the Centennial Exposition at Philadelphia in 1876 the horseshoes exhibited by the Rhode Island Horseshoe Company excelled all others. They were made by machines invented by C. H. Perkins. All forms of heavy and light shoes for horses and mules—one hundred and sixty styles in all—were made by this company, one of the largest of its kind in the country. In 1890 its stock, which had a par value of $100, was said to be worth $1,000 a share.

THE AMERICAN HORSEWHIP

CHAPTER V

The American Horsewhip

At the meridian of the horse and buggy age over ninety per cent of the world's supply of horsewhips came from Westfield, Massachusetts. Twenty million whips were produced there annually, one concern turning them out at the rate of nearly twenty thousand a day. At the turn of the century there were approximately forty firms, employing hundreds of workers, engaged in making whips, whip accessories, and whip-making machinery. In 1910 many of these firms were still going, but not so strongly. A dozen years later the number had shrunk to three. Today there is only one factory in Westfield actively engaged in manufacturing whips, and its output is largely souvenir whips for fairs, carnivals, and circuses.

For almost a century, however, this New England city enjoyed a practical monopoly of the whip business. It became known as The Whip City. It was the boast of its whip-makers that their speed-inducing product saved the world every year several centuries of time. They claimed also that while millions of slaves and others had been whipped since the beginning of the world, it was impossible for anyone to have received a really snapping, stinging, lacerating licking until Westfield began to make whips. Next to tarring and feathering, horsewhipping was considered about the most degrading and outrageous form of punishment one man could inflict upon another. Because it added insult to injury, it was popular during the horse and buggy age as a form of personal and private revenge. Women, of course, were not horsewhipped, except by sadists, drunkards, or villains of the viler sort; but women sometimes horsewhipped men. It is not so many years since an actress, infuriated at the way she had been criticized, invaded the offices of a newspaper in Waterbury, Connecticut, and horsewhipped the dramatic critic. But horsewhipping went out when the Westfield whip-makers were whipped by the automobile, and editors no longer go in fear of the irate subscriber who used to storm into newspaper offices, whip in hand, crying, "Whar is he?"

It is not clear to whom honor is due for starting the whip industry in Westfield. Joseph Jokes is generally credited with making the first whips, the story being that he had a lot of fine quality hickory which he discovered made first-rate whip-stocks. His friends and neighbors to whom he gave pieces of the hickory thought so too, but when they began to come to him regularly for pieces of it, Jokes got the idea that instead of giving his hickory away, he would make it into whips and try to sell them. This was in the year 1808.

Others say the first whips were made by Titus Pease and Thomas Rose in 1801. But whoever is entitled to the credit, the important fact is that the whips, crude as they were they were hardly more than hickory sticks to which horse-hide lashes had been attached—found a market. Others began to make them, and this competition brought about many improvements in the whips, which began to acquire a reputation that spread beyond the confines of Westfield and its encircling belt of towns.

At one period the whip-stocks were boiled in oil. This was supposed to give them added resiliency, flexibility, and toughness. Whips treated in this way were called "twisted" whips. Hickory was not the only wood used, other woods, especially white oak, being popular with the whip-makers. Sometimes the wooden handles were sheathed in sheepskin, the skin being sewn around the stocks.

Then came the plaited whip, which was to set the principle of whip-making in the United States. This was a covering of cotton, silk, or other material, which was woven over the whip-stock from the tip to the butt. It became necessary to cover the whip-stocks, when the centers began to be made of whalebone, with pieces of rattan glued around the bone. Tradition says that D. L. Farnham made the first plaited whip in Erastus Grant's cabinet shop.

At first the Westfield whip-makers followed the English style whip, which was simply a bare stock of holly with a long lash attached to it in such a way that it could be easily detached and replaced by a new lash when the old one wore out. Even the first plaited whips were made on this principle of the detachable lash. Then came the invention by Augustus Black of the straight American whip, which won world-wide popularity, except in England, which adhered to its straight holly whips with long lashes.

The first device for plaiting whips was a crude contrivance. A whip-stock was suspended inside a barrel, butt down, by a pulley and a weight. Smaller weights were attached to the ends of the strands which were to be woven over the stock and these smaller weights hung outside the barrel, and the plaiting was done by hand. Fifteen or twenty strands were used. As the work progressed, the suspended whip was raised higher and higher by means of the pulley and weight, until at length the whole whip from tip to butt was covered.

It was a Connecticut Yankee who really put the infant Westfield industry on its feet. This was Hiram Hull of Windsor. He was brought to Westfield during the first quarter of the nineteenth century by Aaron Phelps, one of the early whip-makers, who had been impressed by Hull when he met him in Windsor. Hull was responsible for numerous inventions and developments of the greatest importance to the whip industry. In Providence he saw a machine braiding shoe laces and bought the rights to it so he could adapt it to the plaiting of whips. Plaiting machines were also imported from England and Germany and developed in Westfield, where eventually all the intricate machinery used in the manufacture of whips was built. The first plaiting machines were operated by cranks or water-power from the Westfield River. Several of the whip factories were located on the bank of the river.

Hull is said to have been the first man to see the possibilities in rattan for making whips. He was watching a vessel from an Asiatic port unload at a dock in New York. In stowing the cargo, rattan had been used for packing, and as the vessel was unloaded the rattan was discarded as worthless—thrown out on the dock for anyone who wanted it. It became one of the basic materials in the making of millions of American horsewhips. At the peak of its producing years the United States Whip Company used on an average six hundred tons of rattan annually, and erected a special brick building for drying, sorting, and storing it. This building still stands behind the wing of the old plant that has been converted by the whip company into a picture theatre.

Under Hull's leadership the whip industry grew rapidly. In 1837 there were thirteen whip factories, employing one hundred and fifty-four men and four hundred and ten women. The value of the product was $153,000. At this time some of the work, such as braiding snappers for the tips of the whips, was done in the homes. By 1855 the number of factories had increased to approximately thirty, with one company alone producing whips of a yearly value of $150,000. Here are some statistics of the leading Westfield whip companies at that particular time.

	Age of Company	Number of Hands	Yearly Value
H. Harrison & Co......	28 yrs.	350	$150,000
William Robinson & Co.	20 yrs.	100	25,000
J. R. Rand Co.	20 yrs.	70	60,000
J. & R. Noble........	20 yrs.	100	50,000
Dow & Gillett........	15 yrs.	100	55,000
Monroe, Brownson & Co.	5 yrs.	30	30,000
R. Loomis & Co........	2 yrs.	15	20,000
King & Avery........	2 yrs.	10	8,000

Twenty-five years later the number of companies had increased to thirty-seven, with a total annual output valued at $880,000, which grew to several million dollars during the best years of the industry. In 1892 there was a merger of fourteen companies into the United States Whip Company, which also owned factories at Windsor, New York, and Sidney, Ohio. The whip factory at Windsor burned during the first decade of the century, and in 1912 the business of the Underwood Whip Company of Sidney was moved to Westfield. In that year, because of price cutting, forty per cent of the whips shipped out of Westfield were ten-cent whips. One company used seventy-five carloads of wood for the butts of its cheap whips. In Westfield it is reckoned that during the great whip-making years 7500 people lived off the whip industry, this figure, of course, representing not only those actually engaged in the business but their families as well.

Hiram Hull's son, David C. Hull, spent all his life as a whip-maker in Westfield and witnessed the rise and

fall of the industry. In 1910, when he was eighty-one
years old, he was one of the oldest whip-makers in
America. Father and son between them were connected
with the whip business for almost a century.

Whip-making involved many different operations.
A straight carriage whip of good grade had a center
composed of rawhide and rattan. This hide was tanned,
dried, and twisted, and run through a machine which
cut and shaped it. Around the rawhide, which was about
the thickness of a pen or pencil, eight pieces of previously prepared rattan were glued and bound in place
until the glue dried. The glued strip of rawhide and
rattan was then rounded and tapered by machinery
and passed along to an experienced whip-maker, whose
job it was to take out the "jumps." Holding the partly
finished whip by the handle, the whip-maker tested it
to see if it bent evenly. If it did not, the whip had a
"jump" in it, which the whip-maker took out with
a plane. An expert workman knew instantly by the feel
of a whip exactly where the "jumps" were, and by a
few deft applications of his plane here and there quickly
eliminated them.

To give a good whip the proper weight and balance
a piece of iron called the "load" was placed in the butt.
The large whip companies used as much as a hundred
tons of iron a year for loading butts.

When a whip had been shaped and tested it was, if of
reasonably good grade, given a covering of rubber,
which made it waterproof. It was then sent to the plaiting machine for its final outer covering. After that it
was filled and given several coats of varnish, and the

mountings—buttons, ferrules, etc.—were added, and, last of all, the snapper. One factory specialized in whip-mountings, making them for all the whip manufacturers, and it is perhaps worth noting that there was even a company in Westfield that made whip-sockets for the carriage trade.

Some of the fancy whips had elaborate mountings with chased buttons or head-mounts and as many as sixteen ferrules of nickel, silver, or gold. Rubber caps were sometimes used on the butts, though most whips had simply buttons of japanned metal. Hand-plaited leather buttons and ferrules were also used. There was as much variety in the mountings as there was in the styles of the whips.

The snaps or snappers were made separately and put on by hand in all the better grade whips. They were of cotton, silk, half and half, or buckskin, and were hand braided or machine made according to the quality of the whips on which they were used. Attaching them was a simple operation, because in plaiting a whip a loop was made at the end of the lash through which the snapper was slipped and secured. A feature of the more expensive whips was the imported handmade English snappers. The snappers on the cheap whips were not made separately, but were all of a piece with the plaiting, an attenuated extension of the lash. They were known as Boston snaps, while the others—the loose snappers—were called Philadelphia snaps.

Most of the rawhide and rattan used in making whips came from India, as did also the water buffalo hide that was used. One whip company stated in its catalogue, "Our rawhide centers cannot be equalled by anybody. We tan our own hides and make our own centers, and use nothing but the best commissariat hides, bought from the English army, cured in the best manner possible, imported direct by us, and use no slaughters, derbungas, or deads, which are inferior stock." This statement was made in connection with a line of rawhide whips, one of which was called the Madras Rawhide, another the Burma Rawhide, and still another the Ceylon Rawhide. "We invite the closest examination," the statement continues, "and do not fear the knife if you wish to cut the whips open." What person whose youth was spent during the horse and buggy age does not remember cutting up old horse-whips just to see what they were made of? And what man of middle age does not recall using an old whip stock for beating carpets?

Whalebone made excellent whips, but was more generally used during the earlier years when it cost only thirty or thirty-five cents a pound than it was later. It rose in value until toward the close of the horse and buggy period it was ten dollars a pound. Despite the high price, many carriage whips continued to be made of whalebone, but they were only one-third, one-half, or seven-twelfths bone. Bone track whips, chiefly in the three and three-quarter foot size, are still made in Westfield.

"The whalebone comes from San Francisco and is cut in New York," one of the old whip manufacturers who is still on the job told me recently. "There are no bone cutters in Westfield now and there's only one man in New York who knows how to cut whalebone for whips."

Nobody knows how many different style whips were made in Westfield. A great variety of materials in all kinds of combinations was used, and the different classes of whips showed many variations in length, color, mountings, and other details of manufacture. The last catalogue of the United States Whip Company, issued some years ago, lists one hundred and forty styles, but actually some two hundred were carried in stock, and this was after the decline had set in. The salesmen of this company carried about sixty sample whips to show to the trade. Their samples included such whips as "Giant Cracker. Full Stock Imported Java. Loaded." "Blue Belton. Combination of Steel Wire and Finest Manila Reed." "Dictator. Solid Rawhide Center." "Park Pride. Warranted Waterproof. One-half Whalebone." "Rough and Ready. Rawhide from Snap Through Cap. Double Wire Undercover." "The Flail. Eel Skin Lined," etc. These were the straight whips, and there were many with long drooping lashes, the drop tops, as they were called, in a variety of styles, including carriage, cab, coach, and express drop tops. The Franklin Whip Company of Westfield imported holly wood stocks and specialized in making long-lashed English whips. The longest whips were the harvester whips, made expressly for use in driving the great teams of horses employed on the harvesting machinery in the West. These whips had ten- or eleven-foot stocks of bamboo or hickory, with lashes four or five feet long.

Literally hundreds of different style whips were manufactured by the Westfield factories.

The best selling whips were the twenty-five- and fifty-cent carriage whips, followed by the better grade of whips at a dollar, a dollar and a half, and two dollars. Some whips sold for as little as five or ten cents, others for as much as twenty or twenty-five dollars. There was really no limit to what you could pay for a fancy whip. A whip with a carved ivory handle cost the purchaser for the handle alone at the rate of a dollar an inch. The handle ranged anywhere from eight to eighteen inches in length. Many whips were made with the owner's name woven into the handle. This gave work to a number of women, but today there is only one woman in Westfield who knows how to do this, and she is seldom called upon to do the weaving for a name whip.

All the manufacturers sold racks for the display of whips in shops and stores. These racks were either straight, cross, or circular, and were usually of the type that was suspended from the ceiling or wall, the whips hanging from them by their snaps. It ruined a whip to keep it standing against a wall.

A picturesque figure during the horse and buggy days was the street whip-seller. He usually chose for his pitch a place beside one of the important public watering-troughs to which horses were being driven to drink. With a whip in one hand and a bunch of colored snappers, like a small bouquet of flowers, in the other, and clutching a bundle of whips under his arm or hugging it to his breast, he would stroll among the wagons and carriages, selling whips to the drivers while they watered their horses. If a horse needed to be unchecked before drinking, the whip-seller stood ready to perform this small service and save the driver the bother of getting down.

One street whip-seller I remember plied his trade for years at the north end of the South Green in Hartford. A large cylindrical tank stood out in the street at the head of the Green, where four streets met. Two of these thoroughfares were used by people driving to town from Rocky Hill, Wethersfield, Berlin, Newington, Elmwood, and other points to the south and southwest, and there was always a horse or two, often more, at the tank. Winter and summer the Jew whip-seller was on hand. He wore a hat that was much to big for him, a pair of blue goggles, and a long coat or duster, depending on the season. On May Day he changed his heavy winter hat with its earlaps for a large, broadbrimmed, farmer's straw hat, which one could not help suspecting was worn as a bid for the agricultural vote. Certainly in his long duster and country hat he looked the traditional stage rube, minus the chin-whiskers.

But the real masters of the art of whip-selling were those one saw at New England county fairs and cattle shows. They knew how to show their whips. There was nothing they could not do with a whip. If you tried to do what they did when you got home with one of their whips, you were sure to break it. I recollect as a boy being held spellbound by one of these whip-sellers at the Cummington Cattle Show. He stood on a platform, a fine figure of a man, with a large black hat, generous handle-bar mustache, stiff-bosomed shirt and low-cut vest, black tailed coat, and striped trousers. He had brought his whips in long round leather cases that he telescoped one on top of the other so as to form a pillar or post of leather which he lashed furiously when showing the quality of a whip. He had a magnificent voice and you could hear him all over the place cracking jokes and whips. So spellbound was I, and so long did I stand in the front row watching him, that at last, to the amusement of the crowd, he gave me a whip to go away.

In this age of motor-cars one never sees men with horsewhips standing or walking about the streets, but formerly farmers and others who used to drive to town behind horses had the habit after hitching their animals of carrying their whips with them as they went about their business. An old catalogue of the paintings in the Wadsworth Atheneum Gallery in Hartford, after stating that the pictures were not to be fingered, says, "Umbrellas, Parasols, Canes and Whips to be left at the head of the stairs."

SLEIGHS AND SLEIGHING

CHAPTER VI

Sleighs and Sleighing

A SINGLE small town in the hills of central Connecticut produced substantially all the sleigh-bells used in
America during the nineteenth century. Thousands of
sugar barrels filled with them were shipped out of the
town of East Hampton, where at one time half a dozen
concerns were engaged in making sleigh-bells. The
largest of these foundries, in which the bulk of the
sleigh-bells was made, still exists. Owned and operated
for over a century by the same family, sleigh-bells are
made there today, though barely enough to say so, since
almost the only purchasers are the Indians on the government reservations, who use them in their ceremonial
dances.

The pioneer American sleigh-bell maker was William
Barton, who was born in Wintonbury, now Bloomfield,
Connecticut, November 26, 1762. During the Revolu-
tionary War he lived in Springfield, Massachusetts,
where his father worked as a gunsmith. After the war
the family returned to Wintonbury. In 1790 young
Barton went to New York and devoted himself to mak-

ing andirons and brass articles. In 1818 he returned
to Connecticut and began the manufacture of sleigh-
bells in East Hampton, then a parish in the town of
Chatham. There had been a forge there for some time
on the stream just below Lake Pocataupaug. Barton's
sleigh-bells differed from other sleigh-bells in that he
was the first to cast them in one piece. The earlier
method was to make them in two parts and solder the
pieces together. He also introduced the method of polishing bells by rolling them in a barrel. He left East
Hampton in 1826 and settled in Cairo, New York, but
twenty years later returned to East Hampton, where he
finally died July 15, 1849. His descendants were active
for many years in the bell-making industry in East
Hampton.

About two years after William Barton went to Cairo
he was joined by a young man from East Hampton
named William Bevin, whose father had bound him to
Barton for the last year of the youth's minority. It was
stated in the indenture, which is still in the possession
of the Bevin family, that when his time was up William
Bevin should be free to copy anything he had learned to
make under Barton. On returning to East Hampton,
young Bevin lost no time in setting himself up as a
sleigh-bell maker.

In 1832 he began to take his brothers into partnership, the firm, in addition to sleigh-bells, also making
waffle irons, coffee mills, pots, and kettles. The small
shop in which the Bevin brothers—William, Chauncey,
Abner, and Philo—started their business is standing
among the buildings of the large plant that sprang up

around it when they became the leading sleigh-bell
makers of the world. The granddaughter of William
Bevin has in her attic the trunk in which her grandfather carried his sleigh-bells when he took the steam-
boat at Middle Haddam to sell his bells in New York.
Other members of the family operate the factory and
make all kinds of bells, from tiny turkey bells to ship
bells. All the bells for the liner *Manhattan*, for example, were cast in the Bevin Brothers' foundry by some
of the same men who made sleigh-bells in the days when
their pleasant jingle was heard in the land.

Many different patterns were used in sleigh-bell
making. The commonest were the globe, band, and rim
bells, which were either single- or double-throated; that
is, the bells had a single slit in them to let out the
sound, or two slits cut across each other at right angles.
The bells were given a simple polishing, or a silver-
white finish, or were plated with nickel, brass, silver, or
gold. The Bevin Brothers made twenty different sizes
of common sleigh-bells, ranging in diameter from seven-
eighths of an inch to three and three quarter inches.
Strung together in clusters of a dozen, they were sold
by the pound as loose bells or were wired or riveted to
neck straps, body straps, or martingale straps. The
number of bells on a strap depended on the size of the
bells used. A body strap might have as many as sixty
small bells, or a fewer number of larger bells of a single
size, or assorted sizes. The price of a strap of sleigh-
bells ran from a dollar to eighteen dollars, depending
on the quality of the harness leather used and also the
quality of the bells with which it was equipped.

The best sleigh-bells were cast from pure bell metal composed of tin and copper, the core of the bell being embedded in the sand when the mold was made. The cheap bells were stamped out of steel or brass.

The difference between the two classes of bells in both tone and volume of sound was made plain to me when Mr. Gordon Bevin, who showed me over the old sleigh-bell factory, jingled first a strap of stamped bells and then a strap of cast bells. The cast bells had a sweeter tone which carried farther than that of the stamped bells.

This difference was also noticeable in the chimes, the open-mouthed bells made to attach to the shafts of sleighs. Chimes were hung in metal frames on top of the shafts or were suspended underneath. They came in many different shapes—tea-bell, hand-bell, gong, band, bevel, beaded, dome, Swiss, etc. The Swiss chimes were cup-shaped. The fanciest were the Russian saddle chimes, which, as the name implies, were not made for the shafts or poles but for attaching to the saddles. Hame chimes were similar to the saddle chimes, except that they were made to be fastened to the hames of the collars rather than to the saddles. Sometimes body straps of ordinary sleigh-bells were made with chimes at the top. Then there were the featherweight speeding chimes designed expressly for fast driving where light chimes were required. The bells were small and occupied a position so close to the under side of the shaft that there was no danger of the horse cutting himself while racing or in case of an accidental fall.

Sleigh racing was a great winter sport in New England. In towns and cities everybody who had a good horse came out for the impromptu cutter races, which never failed to draw a crowd of interested spectators. A broad street free from car tracks, with not too many cross streets or blind corners and with a minimum of heavy traffic, made the best informal speedway. Such a street was Washington Street in Hartford during the elegant Eighties and gay Nineties. With its immense old elms and spacious houses, some of the latter dating from the eighteenth century (one of these, the Charles Noel Flagg house, had a secret hiding place), others with the porticoed fronts of the Greek revival period, and still others with the towers, cupolas, porte-cochères, and battlements of the Victorian era, Washington Street was one of the finest streets in New England. Senators, governors, judges, and other notables lived there. But progress got it and today it is a treeless street of motor-car showrooms, filling stations, and barrack-like apartment houses, differing in no way from similar streets in a hundred other cities.

In the days of cutter-racing there were few more ex-hilarating sights than that of a group of three or four fast horses, "their steaming nostrils white with frost" and the snow flying from their feet as they came smoking along under the giant elms of Washington Street, their sleigh-bells jingling briskly. Men in sealskin caps and dogskin gloves drove their own horses, and many a coachman, unknown to his employer, contrived to drive around to the speedway, perhaps with a horse he had been quietly conditioning, in the hope of indulging in a brush or two in the keen air. Everybody knew everybody else and his horse and there was the deepest interest in the various local rivalries.

A sleigh slipped over the ground so easily that it always seemed as if you were going much faster than was actually the case. This may account for some of the absurd stories told of the time made by horses over snow and ice. Half miles were seldom made in a minute, nor miles in 2:15 time. The only way this could be done, according to one writer, was by marking the end of the course with a piece of brush which would blow in the direction of the horses as they trotted toward it. In Boston in the mid-Eighties a prize of a fine horsewhip was offered for the fastest time made by a horse and cutter over the Beacon Park course. The best Boston horses competed in these trials, but the fastest time was 2:30. Horses never made such good time over snow or ice as over dirt, because no matter how hard or well packed the footing might be, there was always some slippage. The snow and ice yielded to the sharp shoes of the horses. On a dirt track the delicate hoofs of a race horse slide forward several feet in every mile. For some reason faster time could be made over ice in a sulky than in a sleigh.

The rivers of New England afforded fine speedways when they were frozen, and ice-racing was very popular. This was particularly true along the Connecticut River. The sleighs were loaded into pungs and taken down to the river, and the horses, which had been specially shod were led gingerly down the bank. The sport was a dangerous one. Not only was there the risk of the horses falling on the ice but of the animals wounding

themselves with their racing shoes and of being over-
driven. It was the easiest thing in the world to over-
drive a horse while sleighing.

After heavy falls of snow the country highways of
New England often had to be broken out by oxen.
Whittier speaks of this in *Snowbound*. Oxen were far
better than horses for getting through snowdrifts;
they could, in fact, get through snow that was impass-
able to horses. Slow as they were, they always somehow
managed to muddle through the worst drifts, pushing
and treading their way along without lifting their feet
and floundering as horses are apt to do in deep snow.

When the sleighing was good the pastime of many
children after school and on Saturdays was hooking
sleigh rides. The best sleighs for this were the long, low,
flat ones. Seated on the tail end of one of these sleighs
you were out of reach of the driver's whip, and by
changing from one sleigh to another you could ride all
over town. Some drivers did not mind your riding with
them, while others did not know it. For the procedure
was, if possible, to board a passing sleigh unnoticed
by the driver. You stood beside the way in apparent un-
concern, but in reality you were watching your chance
out of the corner of your eye. Once aboard a sleigh, it
was a simple matter, if the driver was mean and forced
you to abandon riding with him, to roll yourself into
a ball and roll off into the snow. The driver who happened to be going up a hill on which there was coasting
was certain to have a load of kids and a string of sleds
in tow before he got to the top. And stealing rides was
by no means confined to children. In Northampton the

Smith College girls made such a practice of hooking rides on delivery sleighs up and down Elm Street that the college authorities had to put a stop to it.

Then there were the straw rides, particularly on moonlight nights, when a dozen or fifteen couples, sometimes more, would nestle in the straw in the bottom of a great sleigh heaped with blankets and buffalo robes and would drive out to some country inn for doughnuts and coffee and old-fashioned square dances. On the way there was always singing and blowing of tin horns, and sometimes the sleighing party was the recipient of a few snowballs flung by boys who were out late coasting. The chaperon sat at the head of the sleigh in the shadows behind the driver and the choice seats were at the other end of the sleigh as far as possible from her. Large pungs were often used for these sleigh rides, though at some livery stables it was possible to charter one of those enormous boat sleighs drawn by six or eight horses and capable of accommodating anywhere from a score to half a hundred persons.

In Longfellow's tale, *Kavanah*, there is a letter, purporting to be written by a schoolgirl to a friend, in which there is the following mention of an old-fashioned New England sleighing party. "Last week we had a sleigh ride, with six white horses. We went like the wind over the hollows in the snow;—the driver called them 'thank-you-ma'ams,' because they made everybody bow. And such a frantic ball as we had at Beaverstock! I wish you had been there! We did not get home till two o'clock in the morning; and the next day Hester Green's minister asked her if she did not feel the fire

of a certain place under her feet, while she was danc-
ing!"

Pleasure driving in sleighs pre-dated pleasure driving in wheeled vehicles. In sleighing one was not handicapped by the quaggy roads, which so often made
riding in carriages an unpleasant adventure. Nor did

THE COURTING SLEIGH

sleighs cost so much as carriages, and this fact, coupled
with the further fact that New England had long winters, accounted for the presence of a sleigh in many
barns long before a buggy, carryall, or other pleasure
vehicle found a place there.

Sleighs were not built to a single pattern but came
in almost as many styles as did carriages. One I admired in my youth was an elegant goose-neck sleigh,

which bore a strong resemblance to one of those swan boats that sailors used to hire for rides on the pond in the Public Gardens of Boston. It had an extra dash of screening as an added protection against the horses flinging snow in the face of the sleighers. On the back of this sleigh was some quaint gold stenciling like that seen on Hitchcock chairs, a Horn of Plenty in a border, and the coachman who drove the sleigh looked like Uncle Sam.

Gideon Welles, Lincoln's Secretary of the Navy, had, appropriately enough, a gunboat sleigh, which he used to drive over the Connecticut countryside.

It was much easier to tip over in a sleigh than in a carriage. The hack sleighs—hacks with their wheels removed and runners substituted—were apt to be top-heavy, and timid women would not ride in them when the going was rutty and uneven.

Not so long ago a friend of mine, who is not old enough to remember the sleighing days, decided he would see for himself what sleigh-riding was like. In the family barn was an ancestral cutter, perfectly sound after all these years. He got it out and, hiring a horse, hitched it to the sleigh and started off merrily enough. But he did not know that you cannot back a sleigh, and in attempting to do so split the heirloom from stem to stern.

Sleighs with their cut-in dashboards were the first streamlined means of land transport. The purpose of the curved dash, however, was not to lessen the wind resistance but to keep the buffalo robes snug about your feet.

The most thrilling of all New England sleigh rides
was the so-called "Nantucket sleigh ride," which, it
will be remembered, was the ride the whalemen of Nantucket were taken for in their open boats over Arctic
seas when they had set their iron in a whale.

GRAIN DEALERS AND GRIST-MILLS

CHAPTER VII

Grain Dealers and Gristmills

Five old women mending grain bags in a dilapidated brick warehouse overlooking a flagged courtyard. That is one of my earliest recollections of the horse and buggy age. The women wore pieces of white flour sacking tied around their heads and aprons made from meal bags. They used darning needles of an astonishing size, and cut patches with monstrous scissors. They were hedged about with piles of mended and unmended bags. On one pile in a corner a cat nursed her kittens. Another cat dozed by the stove. On the window ledge beside one of the women a big yellow tom sunned himself and watched three plump pigeons strut about the court below, picking up grain from the flags. It was part of the old women's job to look after the cats that caught the rats that gnawed the holes in the grain bags.

How many years the five old women sat sewing in the warehouse or how many thousands of bags they

salvaged, I do not know, but it must have been a good
many. They worked for a firm of wholesale grain merchants, of which my father was one of the partners, and
I know that they were paid at the rate of $1.25 a day.
I have heard my father say that one of the old women
could repair as many as a hundred bags in a day. This
must have meant a considerable saving to the firm. Bags
were expensive, especially the long meal bags, and the
firm used lots of them. It did a milling in transit business, its mills having a capacity for grinding 7500
bushels of corn a day, and every year several hundred
thousand new bags had to be purchased.

Besides their mending and cat-tending, the old
women's only other duty was to clean and dust the
office every morning. When I became old enough to
serve summer terms as office boy to the firm, I often
found them at their cleaning when at eight o'clock I
began going the rounds filling inkwells. There was a
row of high, old-fashioned desks at which the clerks
stood or sat on tall stools. The easiest inkwell in the
row to fill was the head book-keeper's, because he was
a little man and had a specially built platform in front
of his desk so he could stand up to his work. My impression of the grain business then was that the men in it
were marvelous penmen. Most of the correspondence
was written in longhand and it was my job to copy the
letters in a hand press. It was the boast of the clerks
that the firm's books were the most beautifully kept
books in town, with the possible exception of the gas
company's books.

My father, who spent twenty-five years building his

business up and twenty-five years watching it go down, knew every grain dealer and gristmill in half the New England states. Many of these grain men owned mills which had been in their families for generations. They knew in the spring precisely where the trout lay in their mill streams, and in the autumn they knew from reports of farmers coming to mill just where the partridges were most plentiful. And every spring my father would go off for a week or two of fishing and every fall for a week or two of hunting. At other times we had many presents of fish and game from country mill owners.

One of my father's friends was Hiram G. Hill, who owned the gristmill on Mill River in Williamsburg, Massachusetts, where on May 16, 1874, there was a terrible disaster. Two or three miles above Mr. Hill's modest mill dam a large dam was built across the valley to store water for the factories and mills in the towns along the river below Williamsburg. An extensive reservoir was created, but the dam was defective and burst. There had been rumors that it was unsafe, and just before it crumbled, the gate-keeper, seeing that it might go at any moment, went out at the risk of his life and opened the gates in an effort to relieve the pressure. He had no sooner done so and got safely back when the breast of the dam broke and the pent-up waters went out with a terrific rush that carried death and destruction for miles down the valley. Ahead of the flood rode Collins Graves on horseback to warn the inhabitants in the valley to fly to the hills. He saved many lives, and his ride was celebrated in a poem of many lines by John Boyle O'Reilly, from which I quote only the last lines:

When heroes are called for, bring the crown
To this Yankee rider: send him down
On the stream of time with the Curtius old;
His deed as the Roman's was brave and bold,
And the tale as noble a thrill awake,
For he offered his life for the people's sake.

Despite Collins Graves' heroic effort, approximately one hundred and seventy persons lost their lives in the flood. The destruction of property was enormous. Sitting in Mr. Hill's house, which I believe still stands on the slight elevation across the road from the mill, I listened many years ago to his experience in the Mill River disaster.

"I heard the noise," he said, "and looked out the window. The first thing I saw was a horse struggling in the lower branches of a tree. I looked across at the mill and saw the miller come out on the platform. He looked up at the wall of water and the wreckage it was carrying and stepped off right in front of it. The next instant he was engulfed. I thought the house was going, but there was a big tree in front which protected it considerably. The house slid back against two other trees which held it. Two men from the mill who had been hauling grain from the depot were coming back with a cart-load when they saw the flood coming. They unhitched the horses, got on them, and raced for the high ground. They won, but we never found any trace of the wagon. There was an appalling dearth of coffins."

The sequel came just before Christmas when another

dam on the same stream broke. It was not so large a
dam as the one that sent Collins Graves on his ride, nor
was there anywhere near so much water behind it, but
people were scared, and word was sent to my grandfather in Northampton to ride and spread the alarm in
the direction of Florence and Leeds. He was not convinced that there was any real danger, but to be on the
safe side he got on his horse and went. There were no
serious consequences, and a few days later a crowd of
his friends got together and for a joke presented him
with a large, round leather medal, now in my possession. On one side within a border is a saddle horse, be-
neath which is the line, "Let the poets sing on."
Stamped on the reverse is this inscription: "Presented
to Capt. E. C. Clark by his friends, as a slight token of
their appreciation of his heroic conduct on the morning
of that dam disaster, which occurred at Haydenville,
Dec. 19, 1874, when, but for his daring bravery and a
scarcity of water, many lives would undoubtedly have
been lost, especially children."

A grain man whom I like to recall is the miller of a
vast, rambling, dusty, brick mill which overhung a river
in the midst of a New England city and by the irony of
fate became a garage before its ultimate destruction.
On hot summer days the miller used to sit in the dark,
cobwebby mill office with his bare feet in an old iron
safe. Late in the afternoon he would drag his chair out
on to the platform above the mill dam and sit tilted
against the wall. Frequently he would wait there to
watch the sunset. I sometimes think the miller, like
Mr. Polly, lived for sunsets.

Nowadays it is not so much the abandoned farm that is conspicuous in the New England landscape as it is the abandoned gristmill. Many of them are falling to ruin beside the streams which once turned their wheels. Mill ponds are disappearing too. With no one concerned to keep either mills or dams in repair, they are rotting away, and soon most of them will be gone, leaving not a trace behind.

"I haven't seen a gristmill in an age," Alfred M. Hitchcock wrote in 1934, in a little volume of privately printed essays entitled *A New England Boyhood*. "Can it be nearly fifty years ago that my uncle took me to mill with him? I suppose it must be. When we arrived, we discovered that the bag of rye brought to be ground had tumbled off the wagon. One has a foolish feeling when he drives up to a mill, and the miller appears at the door, and you 'jolly' him for a minute or two; then you back up to the platform to unload, and lo, you haven't anything to unload. 'You go back and get it, Al,' uncle says; 'you'll find it lying in the road somewhere.' And uncle goes into the mill with the miller while the boy, rather proud to be thus trusted, drives back over the road just traversed, wondering the while whether, when the bag of grain is found, he will be able to lift it.

"No, a gristmill I have not seen in an age. I guess gristmills, at least in this part of the country, are done for. And sawmills are going. It is cheaper to buy Oregon stuff at the lumber yard than to go into one's woods, cut down trees, and haul them to mill. Hundreds upon hundreds of little mills for the manufacture of everything from shoe pegs to clothespins, once busy points in the smaller towns of New England, have disappeared or lie idle. The day of the little mill draws to a close. Large factories have killed the little ones, and

A RHODE ISLAND WINDMILL

these factories, most of them, are run by electric power. Motors have driven out water-wheels."

Not all the New England gristmills were driven by water-power. Windmills were in use down to a relatively short time ago at Nantucket and on Cape Cod

and in Rhode Island. Like the tide-mills, a few of which
may still be found on New England shores—there is
one at Boothbay Harbor, Maine, and another at Ken-
nebunkport—the windmills could not be depended upon
to grind corn whenever a person wanted it ground. The
miller had no control over the winds of heaven. But
windmills were admirably suited to places where water-
power was scarce. While a few have been preserved—
Agnes Edwards Rothery, the writer, lived in one on
Cape Cod for many summers—most of the windmills
have vanished.

Gone, too, are the grain and feed stores, once a
prominent feature of our towns and cities. They have
disappeared almost as completely as the harness shops,
the livery stables, and the blacksmith shops. In the New
England city in which I live there is not now a single
one of these places left in the whole length of Main
Street, where formerly there were seven. Bales of hay
and straw, bags of grain and barrels of flour, stood outside the doorways of the feed stores, and passersby used
to pluck straws from the bales, which were also popular
with dogs, but for another purpose. Just inside the
door of a feed store I knew was a whip socket in which
a horsewhip was kept purposely for driving away dogs
from the bales ranged along the broad brownstone step
that extended across the front of the premises. Today,
I doubt if the retail grain dealer would be allowed to
advertise with the outdoor displays he always used to
have. Retail business in general has retreated from the
sidewalks of New England cities. There is no longer
any carriage trade demanding curbstone service.

The grain stores always had wide doorways to permit the hand-trucking in and out of bales, barrels, and bags. At one side of the entrance there was usually a partitioned off place for an office, with pans of grain samples in the window. Cards stuck in the grain indicated what the samples were—"No. 2 White Oats," "No. 1 Yellow Corn," "Spring Wheat Bran," "Fancy

A GRAIN ELEVATOR AT HARTFORD, CONNECTICUT

White Middlings," etc. Pictures of famous race horses, advertising different patented feeds, adorned the walls. And there was the inevitable lithograph of Rosa Bonheur's *The Horse Fair*, likewise an advertisement for a horse food, which was as standard with feed stores as *Custer's Last Stand* was with saloons.

The feed store was not so dusty a place as the gristmill. One of its virtues was that from it you could get a breath of country air, which was very refreshing to a town dweller in February when the city palled. Haystacks placed in city parks and squares during the winter might be a good substitute, though hay fever victims doubtless would protest.

In the spring a grain dealer's children were in clover when the circus came to town if their father was the lucky one who succeeded in selling the circus the fodder for its animals. Passes never failed to accompany a circus order for hay and oats.

LIVERY STABLES, PUBLIC CARRIAGES AND EXPRESSES

CHAPTER VIII

Livery Stables, Public Carriages, and Expresses

WHEN Ralph Waldo Emerson lectured in the vicinity of Boston he used to ask for a fee of ten dollars and a feed for his horse. The baiting of transient horses formed a considerable part of the business of many livery stables, especially in towns and cities that were centers of country trade. Country folk driving to town for the day would park their horses in a stable, where they would be watered and fed for twenty-five cents. The stables which got the largest share of this business were the ones that were centrally located. A livery stable which stood behind the United States Hotel in Hartford, Connecticut—you needed a compass and a map to find your way around inside this ancient hostelry—did a flourishing business, because in the stable yard there was a snug little drinking place, a hole in the wall with a bar not over five feet long. For the people who did not want to have their horses baited at a stable, many New England towns provided public tie-racks with feed troughs. On Saturdays these places were lined with horses and carriages.

No small part of the livery business was boarding horses for private owners. Four dollars a week was the usual charge for feeding, grooming, and stabling a horse, this figure covering also the washing of the owner's carriage, buggy, or business wagon. Little or nothing was charged for the storage of a sleigh. Occasionally liverymen took liberties with their boarded horses. If they knew the animals were not going to be used by the owners, and all their own horses were out in service, they were not above accommodating a livery customer with a boarder. This was most likely to happen when a large funeral or other unusual event made extraordinary demands upon the resources of a stable, though sometimes the liveryman did not have this excuse. I shall never forget the wrath of a man with whom I was talking on the street one day when he recognized his horse between the shafts of a passing cab.

Livery stables run in connection with hotels and inns had to have ample stabling to care not only for their own horses but also for those of their guests. Some of the largest livery stables in New England were operated in conjunction with summer hotels in New Hampshire and Vermont, a number of these keeping as many as a hundred horses for hire. At the smaller country hotels and inns one frequently met with this slogan emblazoned on the signboard: "Food and Shelter for Man and Beast." The customary charge for oats, hay, and a stall was a dollar a night. At some of these places the benighted traveler was well advised to see that his horse was properly fed when it was put up for the night. For there were a few Yankee innkeepers who were mean enough to cheat a horse of its oats.

The livery stables which catered to transients and rented horses indiscriminately to every Tom, Dick, and Harry who came along sometimes had the misfortune to let their horses to people who did not bring them back. These people were not horse thieves in the sense that they took the horses with the criminal intent of keeping or selling them, but were people who wanted to go places and victimized livery stable keepers in order to get there. It was not so much the loss of the horse hire which troubled the liverymen as it was the bother of recovering their property after it had been abandoned miles away.

A good liveryman did not overwork his horses and would refuse to let them if they had done enough work for one day. But livery horses not infrequently came in for abuse at the hands of customers who did not care what happened to them so long as the animals did not die in their traces while they had them out of the stable. The temptation to pass every vehicle on the road was as strong in the days of the horse and buggy as it is in the present age of the motor-car. Students in college towns were notoriously inconsiderate of livery horses. A Vermont liveryman complained that the presence in his neighborhood of a fast white horse of great endurance had cost him twelve hundred dollars in horseflesh. People driving his livery horses would try to pass or keep up with the white horse, but the livery horses could not stand the pace, with the result that a number of them had literally been driven to death.

The livery business was much better in summer than in winter. New horses were purchased in the spring for use during the good months of the year and sold off in the autumn. A small town livery stable with seven or eight horses would keep only three or four through the winter. The money made from the sale of the others was an important source of income to the liveryman. If he had any knowledge of horses and understood trading, he made a handsome profit buying and selling them. A favorite method was to buy an ailing horse cheap and after curing it sell it for a good price. An old-time New England liveryman told me he once bought a horse in bad condition for seventy-five dollars. He was convinced that the cause of the animal's trouble was eating too fast. He put cobblestones in the manger so as to make it difficult for the horse to get its oats. Forced in this way to eat slowly, the horse was soon cured of its ailments, and the liveryman sold it for three hundred dollars. There were many tricks to the trade. A prospective buyer riding behind a pair of horses might not notice that they were not well matched as to size. If the buyer decided to get out and watch the horses as they were driven past him, the Yankee liveryman would drive the smaller horse on the crown of the road so that the difference in size would be less noticeable.

It was on Sunday that the liveryman wished he had a good string of horses. That was the best day in the

week for the livery business. On Sunday young men
took their girls to ride. The livery business was originally built up chiefly around the so-called courting
buggy. It was never much of a business until young
people took to buggy-riding for pleasure. When roads
were rough and unimproved there was no such thing as
pleasure driving, except in the winter when there was
sleighing. The courting sleigh preceded the courting
buggy. With the improvement of roads and the multi-
plication of light pleasure vehicles, young people soon
discovered that the pleasure they had found in sleighing could be continued in a somewhat different form
through the spring, summer, and autumn, and the
livery stable developed rapidly. It flourished for sixty
or seventy years and then went to seed. But it took
many years to overcome the prejudice against Sunday
driving. The unbending Sunday laws of early New
England which forbade riding or driving on the Sab-
bath, save for purposes of church attendance or in
cases of absolute necessity, lingered on until well into
the horse and buggy age. Even after these laws became
relaxed there were a few liverymen who, as a matter of
principle, would not rent horses on Sunday. In places
where these conscientious men had stables, the liverymen who were not averse to doing business on the Sab-
bath made it a point to state in their advertisements
that horses and carriages could be procured from them
on the Lord's Day.

The old livery stable advertisements show that a lot
of different style carriages were available for hire—
victorias, coupés, surreys, phaetons, buckboards, tally-

ho coaches, omnibuses, hacks, buggies, etc. This was in the larger towns and cities. Small-town livery stables could offer no such array of vehicles. They had no hacks, for example, surreys being used at country funerals.

The liveryman had to exercise reasonable care to see that his carriages and harnesses were in good repair. If a horse ran away and a livery customer was injured in consequence of some defect in a carriage or harness, the liveryman was liable in damages if he knew of the defect or by the exercise of reasonable care could have known. It was also his duty to furnish suitable horses for the purpose for which they were hired. If he negligently furnished a horse that was unsuitable and injury resulted, it was no defense that he did not know it was unsuitable. A horse with the vicious habit of running and kicking was not a suitable horse for a livery stable. (Horne *v*. Meakin, 115 Mass. 326.)

Attempts were made from time to time in the New England courts to have liverymen held to the strictest degree of accountability and to make them responsible for injuries occasioned by their failure to exercise anything less than the highest degree of care. But the courts declined to place them on a par with common carriers of passengers and said that reasonable care was all that was required of liverymen. Said the Supreme Court of Errors of Connecticut, "While the proprietors of stage coaches, hacks and omnibuses, who hold themselves out to the public as general conveyors of passengers from place to place for hire with their own drivers, may be included in the class known as public

or common carriers of passengers, livery stable keepers
whose business is to care for the horses and carriages
of others, and to let their own horses and carriages
either with or without drivers, are not common carriers
of passengers within the legal meaning of the term.
By merely carrying on such a livery stable business
the proprietors of it do not hold themselves out as un-
dertaking for hire to carry indiscriminately any persons who may apply, either to certain places or to such
places as they may desire to be carried. Furthermore,
those who hire carriages from livery stable keepers are
not necessarily conveyed by the vehicles, horses and
drivers chosen by the proprietors, but may in a measure protect themselves by selecting the particular carriage, horse and driver they wish to hire." (Stanley *v.*
Steele, 77 Conn. 688.)

Many livery stables advertised saddle horses for
ladies and gentlemen for hire or sale. Cayuga Chief
was the name of a favorite ladies' hackney in a livery
stable in Worcester, Massachusetts. The horse was a
pacer that one day struck a trot and became distinguished. It was driven a mile to a wagon in 2:38½.
It was claimed for almost every saddle horse for sale in
a New England livery stable that it was a blooded
horse from Kentucky and had taken the prize at the
Illinois State fair. If it balked, it was insisted that this
was an aristocratic tendency. If it shied, it was a direct
inheritance from its great grandfather, the celebrated
race horse. If it was blind in one eye, then there was
just fifty per cent less chance of its shying at objects
in the road. If it ran, it was a matter of blood. If it

picked its feet or bucked, that too worked to its advantage. It was a blooded Kentucky horse and had won the medal at the Illinois State fair.

"The first thing one has to learn when one goes into the horse business," wrote a young lady who bought a saddle horse from a Connecticut liveryman and spent a summer in the early Nineties riding in the state, "is to assume an air of indifference. No matter if horseback riding is the one essential to your health, no matter if your ambition to ride or love of exercise renders the thought of a horseless existence insupportable, conceal your real emotion. What you have got to fight in the man who sells you your horse is a cool reluctance to enter into business relations with you. He'd like to have you have the horse. He likes you, likes the way you talk, likes your looks. If he was not a plain man and no flatterer he'd say he'd rather you have the horse than anybody he ever knew on so short an acquaintance. But there's a little matter between him and a lady over to Willimantic. She's that set on the horse that he'd hardly take the responsibility of disappointing her. But then she hasn't got the figure for it. You've got to have a fine straight figure to look well on a horse, and the Willimantic lady—well, if a man could be excused for plain speech, is a trifle stout, and he has to own he likes a good horse to have—well, a handsome appearing rider. Now if that Willimantic lady *could* be satisfied —Oh, with what weapons will you fight such subtle, subtle flattery!"

The sign of the livery stable was the horse's head, either a painted picture or a carved wooden replica or a stamped metal head similar to those one sees protruding over the horse meat shops of Paris. This sign was usually displayed over the gaping entrance to the stable, or, since many stables were up flagged and cobbled alleyways, it was often the outstanding feature of a sign hung across the mouth of an alley. The liveryman in his printed advertisements, such as his business cards and bill heads, had his choice of many special stock cuts that were part of the equipment of every job printer. A number of the decorations used in this book are from livery stable advertisements found in old New England city directories.

It was also possible to tell a livery stable by the smell. Of all the odors of the horse and buggy age none was so powerful or abiding as that of the livery stable. Some stables, of course, were worse olfactory offenders than others, but it was a difference of degree rather than of kind. They all had an atmosphere that was redolent of damp straw, ammonia, and manure. The ammonia fumes generated by the horses were especially strong on winter mornings after a stable had been closed all night. These fumes were supposed to be harmful to the finish of carriages, but beneficial to persons in poor health, particularly consumptives, who for this reason frequently sought and found employment in livery stables.

Not only did the stables smell, but so did the hacks and cabs that came from them. There was a musty odor about them like that of old carpeted rooms long closed. In damp weather the odor of the horses and harnesses was also quite noticeable. And the drivers not infrequently had breaths that smelled strongly of liquor. All of which sounds most unpleasant, though plenty of people who remember the slower days are of the opinion that the old horsy odors were not nearly so objectionable as are the new oily, gassy, machine smells that have supplanted them.

No one, of course, with any choice in the matter ever chose to live near a livery stable. It was not so much the smell as it was the noise. The trampling of the horses across the wooden flooring was disturbing late at night, and in the small hours the horses sometimes became restless and would stamp or strike the sides of their stalls. Another objection was the flies, which swarmed about a livery stable like bees around a honey pot. The rats, too, were bad. Livery stables were always rather ratty places. And the human element was seldom what it should have been. Stablemen were as a rule a rough, hard set, given to carousing and fighting of a Saturday night or Sunday, to the detriment of the peace and dignity of the neighborhood.

It was these men who were responsible for making livery stables the occasional arenas of the outlaw sport of cock-fighting. Interest in this sport seems to have faded during recent years, but in the horse and buggy age cocking mains were far from rare events. The greatest secrecy shrouded the activities of the cock-fighting fraternity, and the general public knew nothing about the fights, unless the police happened to get wind of a gathering and descended on the devotees of the sport while the feathers were flying and the affair was reported in the newspapers. In one raid some of

the bird fanciers escaped the police by jumping from
the upper window of the livery barn on to a soft muck
heap. One of these men was a breeder of gamecocks
whom I knew. He raised them for a hobby and never
handled any of his birds in a fight. He owned a quaint
sand-glass which he said was used for timing the rounds
of cock-fights in the eighteenth century. It was a
minute-and-a-half glass.

Dog-fights were also sometimes staged in city livery
stables, usually for side bets between the backers of the
dogs. As a boy, I used to cross the street to avoid
passing a fierce bull-terrier that habitually lay, a
scarred old veteran, in the entrance to a cavernous
livery stable not a great ways from my home. A coachman I knew told me that he saw this dog one night in
a prearranged fight, in which the dogs fought almost
noiselessly. A policeman in the street outside the stable
had no inkling of what was going on inside.

Barehanded fist-fights were likewise occasionally held
in livery stables. Some were grudge fights, but many
were fought for the sheer love of fighting. A bruiser
who fancied himself a pugilist would bet he could lick
some other bruiser, and a meeting in some livery stable
would be arranged.

But neither cock-fighting, dog-fighting, nor pugilis-
tic encounters could be said to be common to all livery
stables. Most of them from the point of view of morals
and management were fairly well regulated institutions.

William Dean Howells paid a fine tribute to the public hackmen of Boston. He said that in New York there
were no elderly hackmen, but in Boston they abounded,

and he did not believe them capable of bad faith with travelers. Indeed, he doubted if hackmen anywhere were as predatory as they were painted; but in Boston they appeared to have the public honor in their keeping. The same was true in Portsmouth, New Hampshire. All through New England they seemed to be of native birth, whereas in New York the hackmen were composed of many nations, with a weight in numbers toward the Celtic strain.

Nevertheless, the cities of New England found it necessary from the earliest decades of the horse and buggy age to license and regulate hackmen and public carriages as well as expressmen and expresses. Municipal ordinances established hack and express stands and fixed passenger fares and baggage rates. The charge for the first zone, which was usually from a mile to two miles in extent, was twenty-five cents for each person. Baggage, not exceeding one trunk or ordinary small luggage, was carried without extra charge. Children under four in company with an adult were carried free, and for half fare when between the ages of four and twelve. Fares between midnight and six in the morning were double the ordinary rates. Public carriages for the first hour were $1.50 and sleighs $2.00, each succeeding hour or fraction, $1.00. A hack for a wedding or party cost $3.00. Boys taking girls to a dance would often pool their resources and two or three couples—the normal number of passengers was four—would go together in the same hack. After the ball was over, the lucky couple was the last one in the hack after the others had been dropped at their

homes. Failure on the part of hackmen to comply with
the provisions of the ordinances was punishable by a
fine or revocation of license; while a refusal to drive a
passenger to a remote part of the city meant that the
offender's vehicle would not be allowed to remain on
"a public stand at the cars or boat."

THE PUBLIC HACKMAN

If William Dean Howells had glanced at the animals
attached to the hacks and cabs which he chartered during the course of his New England tour he would have
noticed that in numerous instances the horses, like the
drivers, were elderly. My own recollection of the cab
horses of the period in Boston and other New England

cities is that many of them would not have looked out
of place in a Spanish bull ring. It was, indeed, one of
the stock complaints of the horse age that people never
so much as glanced at the animals between the shafts
of the cabs which they hired. If they would do so, it
was pointed out, and refuse to ride behind broken-down
horses, it would soon become unprofitable to use such
horses and they would disappear from the streets.

The public hackmen, the night-hawk drivers in particular, were often renowned local characters, who in
all but the largest cities knew where everybody lived,
which was helpful to those out late who wanted to go
home but could not remember where they lived. "Never
mind," would come the reassuring reply from the driver
of a sea-going hack. "Get in. I know, anyway."

Very few hansom cabs were used in New England
outside of Boston. The hansom was smart; it was lighter
and speedier than the four-wheel cab or hack, and
many people liked its pleasant bounding motion. But
others thought it uncomfortable and never engaged one
save as a last resort. You certainly had to watch your
step getting into a hansom, and it was too bad if the
horse started just as you were reaching for the handles
with one foot on the step. If perchance the belly-band
of the harness broke, the hansom tilted up and you
found yourself lying on your back, always to the amusement of the crowd.

The pioneer expressman between Boston and New
York was Adolphus Harnden, who was lost with one
hundred and fifty other passengers when the steamer
Lexington burned on Long Island Sound in January,

1840. That year Alvin Adams began doing errands and carrying packages between Boston and New York by way of Norwich, Connecticut. Prior to 1840 most of the express business was done by the post riders, who distributed the weekly newspapers and made small purchases for persons on their routes. The post rider announced his coming to a customer by blowing a tin horn. In 1854 many of the New England expresses were merged into the Adams Express Company. The large, square-topped express wagons of this company will be remembered by many readers of this book. They were made for many years by a wagon-builder in Bloomfield, Connecticut.

Local expressmen and expresses were regulated in the same manner as hackmen and public carriages. For one trunk, valise, carpetbag, bandbox, hatbox, bundle, or other similar package, carried within certain limits, the rate was twenty-five cents. Public express stands were established, customarily at the railroad station and at some central point in the business section. The expresses were open wagons which in summer sported large colored umbrellas over the drivers' seats—orange, tan, green, red, blue, and parti-colored umbrellas, which often bore the name in large letters of the merchant who had donated them to the expressmen for advertising purposes. Under these umbrellas the expressmen, with their wagons backed up to the curb, took naps while stretched out on their wagon seats. Their horses dozed in the shafts, coming to life at noon when the nose-bags were brought out from under the seats. There was much tossing of heads as they ate their oats to the excited chirping of sparrows. The horses standing most of the day in the street naturally made the public express stands untidy places, and on this score the expressmen were sometimes told to move on as a particular stand was discontinued in favor of one in a less prominent location.

THE PRIVATE COACHMAN

CHAPTER IX

The Private Coachman

PEOPLE who do not remember the horse and buggy age must not judge the coachmen of that period by the chauffeurs and taxi drivers of today. The old coachmen were no more like their modern successors than the chantey-singing seamen of the Yankee clippers were like the sailors who nowadays go to sea in motor-driven ships. Many coachmen were better known local characters than the people for whom they drove. They took pride in their appearance and in the appearance of their horses and carriages. They were not so well educated, perhaps, as are our present-day chauffeurs and taximen, but they had loads of that admirable quality—horse sense. No chauffeur ever succeeded in conferring the same social distinction upon his employer that the private coachman did.

Comparatively few coachmen became chauffeurs. Most of them had been around horses too long. They were not easily adaptable to driving horseless carriages.

A man who had spent all his life with horses, feeding them and grooming them and training them and winning their affection, could hardly be expected to have his heart in a job which required polishing and tinkering with senseless machines.

Some people treated their coachmen as they did their old horses, turning them off to end their days under mean conditions of life. Others looked after theirs, keeping them as gardeners or getting them jobs in non-mechanical lines of work such as janitors and watchmen. But a veteran coachman whom I met the other day told me he had sunk to the position of a car washer in a garage—a garage that once was a livery stable. He was cheerful, however, and still dreamed of some day owning a horse.

"In May," he said, "when the weather gets good, I hope to get me a good horse."

I recall the case of another Irish coachman who worked for a family in my neighborhood for over thirty years. He was kept on for several weeks after the horses and carriages had been sold and a new automobile and a youthful Swedish chauffeur installed in the stable. It was a cruel situation, this meeting of the old order and the new, the coachman knowing that his occupation was gone and that he would be going himself as soon as the family plucked up the courage to tell him to go. A quarrel with the Swedish chauffeur was the apparent rather than the real cause of his final dismissal.

"I wish," he said to me during those last days, "them

damn Swedes would go back to Switzerland where they
came from."

This coachman was a leader among the city's coachmen. One year he and his wife led the Coachmen's Ball,
which, like the Firemen's Ball, was an annual affair.
His wife wore a red velvet gown that had belonged to
the lady for whom her husband drove. There was never
any fixed date for the Coachmen's Ball. The Firemen's
Ball was always held the night of Washington's Birth-
day and was usually broken up by some practical joker
turning in a false alarm. Once it was ruined by a brilliant display of the Aurora Borealis misleading the
firemen into thinking that the north end of the town
was in flames. But the coachmen had to watch their
chance and choose a date for their ball when their
services would not be needed to drive their employers
to some social function. The ball was given under the
auspices of The Private Coachmen's Benevolent Association, a corporation that was dissolved during the
World War, after lingering in a state of syncope for
several years before its death.

After the Civil War a number of ex-slaves became
coachmen for New England families. One of these
coachmen whom I remember was Henderson Green, who
had been a slave in Virginia. He had attached himself
to the Gideon Welles family in Washington during
the war and afterward returned with the family to
Connecticut. He acted as body servant for Gideon's
son Colonel Thomas Welles, whenever the latter went on
active service. At one engagement Henry become panic-
stricken and fled when the shooting began, but stopped

when he came to a bridge on which appeared a vision of Mrs. Gideon Welles, motioning him to return and saying, "Go back, Henry, go back!" As he stood in greater awe of her than of the enemy, he returned to his place. After the war Colonel Welles accompanied Admiral Farragut on his cruise around the world and Henry went too.

He remained with the family until his death in 1911 and was buried in the Welles family lot in Cedar Hill Cemetery in Hartford, the only colored person buried in the cemetery, with the exception of a family that slipped past the authorities unnoticed. His burial with the family which he served for three generations gave Henry Green a brief measure of posthumous fame. There was a storm of protest, the Southern press being very emphatic in its view that the color line should be drawn after death as well as before.

Henry who was a short and powerfully-built man, as black as midnight, slept in the usual coachman's room in the Welles' red brick barn, with a huge six-shooter and a rabbit's foot under his pillow. The gun, he said, was for the protection of the chickens; the rabbit's foot was presumably for his own safety. He believed in witches and ghosts and drank kerosene for his rheumatism. One summer night when I was eight and encamped for the night with Gideon Welles' two grandsons, aged seven and nine respectively, in a remote part of the Welles garden, Henry sat on a bench outside the tent door and told us such unnerving ghost stories that when at length he knocked out his pipe and left us we were so badly frightened we all ran home.

In the stable next to Henry was a German coachman named Max, a gnome-like little man with a beard. At one time a beard was an asset to a coachman, the dignity and staidness of a family being judged by the length and fulness of the coachman's beard. In windy weather I have seen these coachmen wearing rubber bands around their beards.

Next door to Max was a tall Yankee coachman, Ezra Trowbridge, who, though probably the laxest coachman on the street, was always on the run, as if he did not have time to do half the things he wanted to in this life. His horses were continually getting loose from their stable and running over people's lawns and cutting them up, but it was a quiet neighborhood, and I think people really liked the excitement of the runaways. Ezra was clever at catching his horses and he was also the best rat-catcher on the street. He trapped rats in his stable with figure 4 traps, which he whittled himself and set with big bars of lead that crushed the guts out of the rats. He could make anything, and I shall always remember him for what he made for me—a toy theatre, complete with tin reflectors for the footlight candles, a turkey red curtain and bell, and a green carpet on the stage.

There were many other coachmen—Terrence Quirk, John Ringrose, Ed Maney, and Ben Horan, to name only a few—whom I remember for kindnesses and favors done me in my youth. But everyone who lived in the time of which I am writing will have his own memories of the coachmen whom he knew.

One of the few writers to pay tribute to the American coachman is Francis Parsons, who says in his book of New England essays, *The Friendly Club and Other Portraits:* "One usually stood rather in awe of the coachman—particularly in boyhood, the period with which he is chiefly associated in the memories of most of us. He was a person of strange and exalted attainment. He held mysterious and telepathic communication with his horses. He understood them and they him. He had theories about shoeing, he could prescribe for most of their ailments, he hissed at them queerly while he groomed them. Moreover, he had the real sporting spirit. He knew all about the performances of Maud S. and John L. Sullivan. He called the firemen and the policemen by their first names, and the fire-bell would send him running out of the stable at any hour.

"If the boy wanted to acquire a puppy," Mr. Parsons continues, "he got the coachman to select and clip its ears (without anesthetic) behind the stable— or, if the coachman was wise, he persuaded a friend to do this surgical work at some livery stable, out of earshot of the family. Probably when the puppy was grown the coachman surreptitiously staged fights with him against rival dogs, chaperoned by brother coachmen, late at night after the boy and his elders were asleep, thus occasionally providing a precarious addition to his wages if the dog came up to expectations. To tell the truth, it was generally selected for its fighting qualities."

A coachman's job was no sinecure. The daily routine was exacting and strenuous. A coachman had to be up early to feed and groom his horses and muck out the stable. There were carriages to be greased and washed and harness to be cleaned and oiled and polished. It took half an hour to groom a horse and about the same time to wash a carriage. A coachman with three horses to look after and the equipment that went with them had his hands full. There was a never-ending succession of details which required attention during the intervals between morning shopping tours and afternoon drives. In addition to the ordinary stable routine, many coachmen also mowed lawns and generally kept up the places where they worked. In the winter they tended furnaces and shoveled snow. For all this the average wage was sixty dollars a month.

It was unusual in New England, outside of Boston or Newport, to see a carriage with two men on the box. The only person, for example, in Hartford, who had a footman was Mrs. Samuel Colt, the widow of the arms manufacturer. Her carriage servants, like her horses, were always well matched, not necessarily in size, but in figure and complexion. It would have been a solecism to put a fat, round-shouldered, red-headed coachman on the box beside a lean, black-visaged groom. Nor did a man with whiskers look well with one who was clean-shaven. Ears, too, were important from the point of view of the person riding in the carriage. Ladies taking the air did not like to ride behind a coachman with abnormally prominent ears.

New Englanders were slow to put liveries on their

coachmen. Just as pleasure vehicles were at first considered ostentatious, liveries for coachmen were thought to be pretentious. All that was supplied to the coachman in the way of apparel was the discarded top hat of the head of the house. I knew a coachman who never wore a silk hat because his boss had such a little head. Whenever his employer went to the hatter's to buy a new hat and was asked what size he wore, he would say he did not know, and as they measured him would quote the lines:

> And still the wonder grew
> How one small head
> Could carry all he knew.

When silver-buttoned liveries came in, some people provided wide-skirted coats for their coachmen, with four buttons in back, two at the waist and two at the tails; while others favored the shorter, straighter coats, with cloth buttons when the family was in mourning. Grooms' coats were shorter than coachmen's coats, had six buttons in back, and no flaps to the pockets. In summer, coachmen were sometimes dressed in light-colored liveries to match the upholstery and fringe of the carriage. In winter many of them wore fur capes. On the whole, coachmen were far smarter in appearance than are the chauffeurs of today.

The general appearance of a person's horses, carriage, and coachman was a reflection of the person's taste. Some people invariably made a fine appearance, everything being correct down to the last detail of the fit of their horses' harness and their coachman's livery. Others did not have the gift. One person who did have it was a prim little old lady who lived in a swell-front brick house with a silver door-plate. To see her being driven around the city you would not suspect that she had a mania for speed, but she always approached her house through a back street, and when this street was reached her coachman would touch up the horses and away they would go. They would tear down that back street, the coachman shouting at the horses, so that people who did not know it was part of the ritual of the lady's drive thought it was a runaway. It was certainly alarming, but the old lady loved it.

Here and there in New England cities, hanging against the walls of old theatres, one may still see the carriage lanterns which were used when people went to the theatre in their carriages. On driving up to the theatre the coachman was given a card bearing a number, and another card with the same number was given to the theatregoer. When the performance was over, the theatre guest would step to the entrance and hand his card to the carriage-crier, who would look at it in the light of the lanterns and call the number. The coachmen on the line of waiting carriages would pick up the cry, echoing it down the street until the coachman holding that number was notified that his passengers were ready. He would then pull out of line and driving up to the entrance, pick them up and take them home.

BARNS AND STABLES

CHAPTER X

Barns and Stables

Many years ago during an unusually high spring freshet the frame of a barn drifted down the Connecticut River to Hartford. It was a stoutly constructed affair, fitted and pegged together. It was found floating in the river by the members of a newly organized religious society which had no meeting house. They considered its discovery as an event of Providential significance and assistance. They secured the drifting "meeting house," placed it on a street corner, and for many years it served as a church.

Today in New England one sees everywhere similar instances of barns and stables being put to uses very different from that for which they were built. Both in town and country they have been converted into antique shops, gift shops, studios, guest houses, and eating places of all kinds. In Boston there is a stable where people lunch and dine in the old horse stalls. One hot

summer day I stopped to eat at a great country barn
in Harvard, Massachusetts, and saw an elderly lady
solemnly eating chicken and waffles while sitting in an
ancient sleigh. I once called on a Boston publisher,
whom I found in the vicinity of Charles Street, living
and carrying on his business in a made-over stable. It
was an attractive and comfortable place. More so, I
thought, than the unimproved coral-colored barn in
which some people I knew used to spend the summer
next to an expanse of mud flats adjoining Massachusetts Bay.

It has become quite the usual thing for barns and
stables to be used for little theatres. Amateur dramatic
societies find them convenient places in which to present bills of one-act plays. Doubtless some members
of these organizations who are in their late forties or
early fifties started their barn-storming careers when
as children in the horse and buggy age they gave shows
in their own barns. The children of the two-car garage
age will never know what they missed by not being able
to play in barns. Louisa M. Alcott said that the hap-
piest days of her life were the Concord days when
plays in the barn were a favorite amusement. How
amusing those plays were can be gathered by reading
them in the book, *Comic Tragedies, Written by Jo and
Meg and Acted by the Little Women.* When Miss Alcott won fame as an author she gave her father a horse
and buggy, which he drove very carefully at the rate
of three miles an hour.

The first stable I knew to be used for a private
library abutted on the old-fashioned New England gar-

den of Henry Barnard, the first United States Commissioner of Education, who was the founder and editor of the *American Journal of Education*. Although he lived in a large brick house, he did not have room for all his books and kept the overflow in the loft of a neighboring stable which he rented from a widow who no longer kept horses. The stable had a postern door that opened on the Barnard garden, and I can remember the old gentleman, with his flowing beard, floppy black hat, dark spectacles, and stick, as he came down the garden path, fumbled in his pocket for the key, and let himself into his stable study. He looked like Walt Whitman at the time they took up a collection to buy the poet the horse and buggy he used to drive around Camden.

Once when Mr. Barnard retired to his loft he left the stable door open, and with youthful curiosity I sneaked up the stairs to see what he was doing. As I made the ascent, cautiously, lest I be found out, not a sound came from him. All that could be heard in the stable was the noisy buzzing of a pair of bluebottles. I began to think that perhaps the doyen of educators was lying in wait for me with his cane at the head of the stairs, but when at last I reached a point from which I could see the library, I discovered the old scholar in a shabby wing chair sound asleep.

Later I was to do considerable reading in another stable library farther up the street. This library was chiefly a fiction library, its reading matter consisting principally of novels of the half-dime variety—*The Liberty Boys of '76, Young and Old King Brady De-*

tectives, Nick Carter, etc. It also contained a store of old magazines, the most popular of which was *The Black Cat*. The library started in the cupola of the barn, access to which was gained by climbing up the side of the hayloft and then crawling out along a beam. As the fame of the library spread and others wished to join, it was moved from the cupola to the unused coachman's room. On the upper floor of most stables a portion of the loft was partitioned off with matched sheathing, to form a room for the coachman to sleep in. If there was no coachman or he lived off the premises, the room made a good boys' club room. For the library it made an excellent winter reading room. A street car stove kept the place warm, and the readers lounged on summer porch furniture stored there for the winter. Smoking was encouraged.

A library more closely akin to the Barnard library was the one in the brick stable of the Adams mansion at Quincy, Massachusetts, in which Brooks Adams kept his books and worked when he was a lecturer at Boston University Law School thirty years ago. He was fond of the bookish retreat he made for himself in the stable, but the rest of the Adams family did not approve of books being kept in such a place.

In the days when people kept horses they placed weathervanes on their barns and stables, and in New England these took a variety of forms, from the traditional rooster or cock to American eagles and horses. On the barns of the tobacco plantations along the Connecticut valley one still sees an occasional vane in the form of a tobacco leaf. Arrows, of course, were and are

common, either plain or with more or less fancy scroll
work. The eagle vanes were always made with arrows
to indicate the direction of the wind. In seaport towns
one saw and still sees vanes in the shape of whales,
ships, gulls, and fishes. Cow vanes, sheep vanes, and
hog vanes adorn many country barns, and I have seen
an old farm vane in the form of a plow. City stables
often had bannerets, sometimes with the initial of the
owner worked into the design. Weathervanes offered a
tempting target to young marksmen, and many an old
vane bears bullet marks.

The horse vanes were the most popular of all. Thousands of them still exist. The one most frequently seen
is a replica of the famous New England Morgan horse,
Ethan Allen, the stallion with the perfect racing form.
A rare Ethan Allen weathervane represents him being
driven to a high-wheel sulky. It was copied from a
Currier and Ives print. The driver has side whiskers
and a short jacket. The horse's hoofs, which do not
touch the bar of the vane, give the effect of the horse
fairly flying over the ground. Made of iron and stamped
sheet metal, with the spokes and shafts of the sulky
and the driver's whip of wire, the vane is a yard long
and eighteen inches high. There is one on a barn close
to the College Highway in Westfield, Massachusetts.
A specimen was shown at the exhibition of American
folk art at the Museum of Modern Art, New York, in
1932. It came from the vicinity of Boston and there
is a photograph of it in the catalogue of the exhibition.

Instead of weathervanes, some people equipped their
barns with lightning-rods. In many localities the light-

ning-rod salesmen seem to have done a thorough job, to judge from the barns that fairly bristle with rods. One of Herman Melville's *Piazza Tales* shows how these men went about New England trading on people's fears. It is the humorous story of a lightning-rod salesman who tried to sell Melville one during a thunderstorm. The author of *Moby Dick* threw him out in the rain.

A number of manufacturers during the horse and buggy age did a thriving business making stable fixtures. For the horse stalls you could get iron or brass caps for the wooden stall posts, or cast-iron stall posts complete with caps; openwork stall guards for the tops of the sides; wrought-iron hay racks and cast-iron mangers, and any number of different kinds of stall drains and gutters. For the harness room there were many special hooks and brackets. Suspended from the ceiling of almost every stable was a bracket for washing and oiling harness. For the carriage house there were such fixtures as racks for robes and poles. Other equipment for the stable included water-troughs, tie rings, hitching bars, whip racks, patent feed bins, and implement holders of various kinds. Among the necessary implements were buckets, brooms, forks, shovels, stall cleaners, brushes, baskets, carriage jacks, hose, shaft supporters, chamois, and many other articles designed to keep horses, carriages, and coachmen in presentable form. From the point of view of equipment and layout probably the finest stable in New England was that of the late Thomas W. Lawson, the Boston financier, at Scituate, Massachusetts.

The persons with the most extensive and intimate knowledge of barns, who, in fact, could be said to be connoisseurs of barns, were the tramps of the horse and buggy age, who plodded along the roads by day and slept in the hay mows of country barns at night. Whittier has told how in the gray of the morning he often used to see one or more of these wanderers emerging from his barn, where they had spent the night. As a boy he was frightened by one of them. "I was once sent to the barn," he said, "to fodder the cattle late in the evening, and climbing into the mow to pitch down hay for the purpose, I was startled by the sudden apparition of a man rising up before me, just discernible in the dim moon light streaming through the seams of the boards. I made a rapid retreat down the ladder; and was only reassured by hearing the object of my terror calling after me, and recognizing his voice as that of a harmless old pilgrim whom I had known before."

Whittier also has told how the advent of these beggars or old stragglers, as they were called, was an event of no ordinary interest in the generally monotonous quietude of New England rural life. "Many of them were well known," he said; "they had their periodical revolutions and transits; we could calculate them like eclipses or new moons. Some of them were sturdy knaves, fat and saucy; and, whenever they ascertained the 'men-folks' were absent, would order provisions and cider like men who expected to pay for it, seating themselves at the hearth or table with the air of Falstaff—'Shall I not take mine ease in mine own inn?' Others, poor, pale, patient, like Sterne's monk, came creeping up to the door, hat in hand, standing there in their gray wretchedness with a look of heart-break and forlornness, which was never without effect on our juvenile sensibilities. At times, however, we experienced a slight revulsion of feeling, when even these humblest children of sorrow somewhat petulantly rejected our bread and cheese, and demanded instead a glass of cider."

Evidently the worst of the lot were the Barrington beggars, a tribe of lazy strollers having their place of rendezvous in the town of Barrington, New Hampshire, whose low vices placed them beyond the pale of most people's benevolence. Not unconscious of their evil reputation, they came in all shapes and with all appearances but their true one. It was particularly vexatious, said Whittier, to discover, when too late, that one's sympathies and charities had been expended upon such graceless vagabonds as the Barrington beggars. New Englanders found it almost impossible to keep them out of their hay mows at night.

Old cobwebbed country barns, weathered to a silver gray or painted a deep rose, with their interior walls flanked by mows of hay from floor to rafters had an aroma and attraction of their own. Mingled with the sweet smell of the hay was the odor of the dried ferns and flowers that formed an inevitable part of the hay harvest. These ancient barns were the scene of many old-fashioned New England husking parties, which were invariably merry gatherings. Lanterns were hung high on pegs, and while some broke the ears from

the stalks, others tore the husks from the ears, and still
others bore the heaping baskets of corn to the granary.
When the last ear was husked a blast from a horn announced supper in the farm-house kitchen, and the
young men and women broke impetuously from the
barn with shouts and laughter, keen for the fun that
was to be the climax of the party.

The horse-sheds which churches built for the protection of the horses and carriages of their members
came in with the coming of wheeled vehicles. Hundreds
of them are still standing and are regarded as quaint
survivals. In their day they were considered disfigure-
ments. They were hardly known before the Revolution,
and many churches did not have them until the second
quarter of the last century. Most of them are distinctly of the horse and buggy period. Built primarily
for Sunday use, the horse-sheds were sometimes a con-
venience on week-days. Once while driving with my
mother in the Berkshires we were surprised by a
thunderstorm in a village in a deep pocket of the hills.
The storm, like ourselves, seemed captured within those
confining hills. It rolled back and forth, becoming fear-
fully violent, and hurling down hailstones the size of
moth balls. But with the coming of the first big drops,
we drove our horse in a swirl of dust around to the
horse-sheds behind the Congregational church and there
sat out the storm; listening to the rain and hail on
the roof and looking at the swallows' nests and at the
tin signs advertising Ayer's Sarsaparilla and different
veterinary remedies, and at the places where the horses,
the Old Billys and Dobbins, billeted there on hundreds

of Sundays, had gnawed the woodwork. When the storm finally slipped away through a gap in the hills and we backed our buggy out of the shed to resume our journey, the sun was shining on the wet but undraggled golden feathers of the weathercock on the church steeple.

FIRE AND POLICE

CHAPTER XI

Fire and Police

EARLY in the evening of May 17, 1895, the great covered bridge which since 1818 had spanned the Connecticut River at Hartford burned in one of the most spectacular fires ever seen in the state. Twenty thousand people lined both banks of the river and watched the old hulk burn, cheering lustily as the flaming spans one by one broke from their piers and tumbled into the river. Built of Connecticut upland pine, the bridge, which was over a thousand feet in length, was of double-barrel construction, with separate lanes or driveways for the eastbound and westbound traffic; and it was in the south driveway of the second span from the East Hartford end that the fire started. Ten minutes after its discovery the entire structure was in flames.

Two horses, the best known pair in the Hartford Fire Department, perished on the bridge. They were attached to a hose cart from the nearest fire-house. This

145

hose cart was the first to reach the bridge. When it arrived the only sign of fire was a little smoke coming from one of the windows at the far end of the bridge. The hose was connected to a hydrant and the transpontine drive to lay the line to the fire began. On reaching the fire the men began to adjust the nozzle of the hose, but were forced to abandon their work when the flames suddenly broke through the roof and flooring, spreading rapidly. Men and horses were surrounded by flames. There was no chance to turn the hose cart around in the narrow lane-way. The horses reared and plunged as the driver tried desperately to get them clear. He had no knife to cut the traces, but he managed to get one trace off, partially freeing one horse. He tried to push the pole up far enough to get them both clear but he could not. The firemen worked to save the animals until their own lives were in peril. When they finally fled, the horses were down, smothering in the smoke and flames, and when the span burned away the cart and horses were plunged into the river. Late at night a man who rowed out near the blackened piers reported finding the cart and horses. Only the horses' ears showed above water.

The loss of that pair of horses was mourned more than the passing of the ramshackle old bridge, which most people were glad to see go. The horses were the pride of the fire department. They were well-trained, affectionate beasts and drew many visitors to the firehouse where they were quartered. After the recovery and burial of their bodies, a thriving trade was done by Yankee hawkers selling burnt horseshoes which they claimed were taken from the dead horses. Obviously the two horses could have had only eight shoes between them, but scores of spurious shoes were sold as genuine relics.

Housed in the same fire station with these horses was Jumbo, the huge steam self-propeller, which was the wonder of the town and the terror of all horses, except the fire horses. It was the tillerman of Jumbo, as the driver of the horseless steamer was called, who taught the horses many tricks, one of which was to stamp out a lighted match. Jumbo itself figured in one of the first silent motion pictures, a short reel showing Chief Henry J. Eaton of the Hartford Fire Department driving his white horse and open buggy to a fire, while behind him, belching smoke and sparks, but with no chance of overtaking the chief's speedy steed, came Jumbo. This movie, like the picture of the Empire State Express running at what was then thought to be the breath-taking clip of a mile a minute, was among the earliest short thrillers of the screen.

Chief Eaton was a veteran of the Civil War, a fire-eater if there ever was one. He swore terribly at fires and many people professed to be shocked by his language, though there were many respectable townsmen who ran to fires chiefly to hear the chief swear. Looking back at those days, I can recall few sights more thrilling than that of the old fire chief in his scarlet-wheeled buggy driving his white horse down Main Street as if the devil were after him. As he flashed by, with the enormous foot gong under the dash of his buggy clanging madly, he seemed to me to be the incarnation of Speed. I suppose he was going at least sixteen miles an hour.

Proud as New England's insurance city was of its fire department and particularly of Jumbo, which gouged holes in the asphalt, set fire to awnings, and once during a parade so frightened the marshal's horse that the unfortunate gentleman came a cropper and died in the gutter of his injuries—proud as Hartford was of Jumbo, it was nevertheless amused when in the winter horses had to drag the monster steam engine through the snow to a fire. But, of course, when snow lay deep in the streets extra horses had to be used to make up "spike teams" for the regular horse-drawn apparatus. This was done by putting one of the regular horses in at the lead and one of the extra horses in at the pole.

When at last the entire fire department was motorized and the horses had made their last run, one of the first alarms came shortly after a snow storm and the new motor equipment made sorry work of getting to the fire. Some of it, if I remember rightly, never did arrive. People who regretted the passing of the fire horses shook their heads and said, "What did I tell you?"

Many stories have survived of the cleverness of the horses in running to fires. The chief's horse, which had the most practice because it went to most fires, was wonderfully proficient in a crowded thoroughfare, pulling up short whenever its progress was blocked and breaking into a gallop whenever there was an opening. But this was characteristic of the horses used by the chief engineers of city fire departments everywhere, particularly in New England, where the horses often had to pick their way through crooked, narrow, and congested streets. Because of the comparative lightness of the chief's buggy or wagon, smaller horses were used for this work than on the engines, hose carts, and hook and ladders. The Boston Fire Department favored for its chief engineer and his assistants the tough, intelligent, short-stepping, Vermont bred Morgan, weighing from 950 to 1050 pounds.

Few horses were any better cared for than fire horses. They were well fed, well stabled, well groomed, well shod, and their feet were always well oiled. But the life of a fire horse was not an easy one and its period of usefulness was limited. The average fire engine with its crew weighed in the neighborhood of four tons, and this extremely heavy load had to be drawn by a team of horses going at full gallop. The work was unique, requiring big horses in the pink of condition. Even with the best of care, the fire horse was good for only seven or eight years' service. There were exceptions, of course. In 1890 the Boston Fire Department, which had about two hundred horses, could boast of a number of veterans that had served the city for a decade. The Boston horses ranged in weight from 1200 to 1600 pounds, with most of them tipping the scales at 1400 pounds. Providence had no fire horses weighing over 1400 pounds. Relatively light horses were sometimes strong enough for the heavy work of the departments.

"One of the best, oldest, and lightest engine horses in Boston," says a writer of the period, speaking of a fire horse used in that city during the Eighties, "is a rather plain, brown fellow, weighing about 1175 pounds, with a short, strong back, splendid shoulders, and stout limbs, with big knees and short cannon-bones. His expression is extremely gentle and intelligent. At present he is the off-horse on the chemical engine in Bulfinch Street, his mate a handsome dapple gray, with flowing white tail. The brown horse is reckoned by the engine men to be twenty-two years old, having been in the service many years. I suspect that there has been some exaggeration in this statement, but he is certainly an old horse. His mate is ten, and considerably larger, but the two step well together and make a fast team. Their driver assured me that he had once given the protective company a fair beating on Washington Street, in a race to a fire."

Heavier horses of this same type—short-legged and strong-backed—were considered best for hauling engines, in which the weight was close to the ground. To ease the strain of starting, some departments used a harness with a strong spiral spring in the trace near the whiffletree. Horses of a rangier type were thought to be best adapted for the hook and ladders, in which the weight was higher. Three horses harnessed abreast were used on the hook and ladders. The hose cart was at first nothing more than the old two-wheel, hand-drawn hose-reel, with shafts for a single horse. Boston introduced the four-wheel hose wagon, but only one horse was used to draw it, and it was not until well into the Nineties that a second horse was added. In the hose carts of the Seventies and Eighties the hose was not

laid in the cart as it is now, but was wound on a large
reel. One of these carts, with its reel and lone horse,
is shown in the bas-relief on the base of the statue of
the Chief of the Pawtucket (Rhode Island) Fire Department, who was killed in 1884 in the discharge of
his duty. The statue, which stands in the square at the
corner of Main Street and Mineral Spring Avenue,
shows the chief in full beard and full fire-fighting re-
galia—old-fashioned fireman's helmet, three-quarter
coat, rubber boots, and speaking trumpet. The manner of his death is depicted in the bas-relief. The hose
cart is tipped over on the chief, who lies half under it
mortally wounded.

The weak point of all fire horses was their feet. That
is where they gave out. The great rough-shod horses
galloping over paved streets with their heavy loads
brought their feet down with gigantic force on the
paving stones. It was this pounding that eventually
broke them down. Every possible care was taken of
their feet, which were kept filled with tar and oakum to
prevent them from becoming dry and hard as a result
of constantly standing on wooden floors, and their hoofs
were kept oiled to promote fast growth. No other horses
cast their shoes with such frequency as fire horses. In
Boston it was expected that at least one shoe would be
thrown by nearly every team of horses that went to a
fire. Frequent re-shoeing was apt to wear away the
hoofs; hence the attention given to their growth. The
only public service horses that wore out faster than the
fire horses were the street-car horses. Six years was
the limit of their utility.

It took the horse-drawn fire apparatus a surprisingly short time to get started for a fire when the alarm sounded. The horses were harnessed and on the way in less than half a minute, usually in fifteen or twenty seconds, sometimes less. The horse stalls with their windowed doors were ranged across the rear of the firehouse behind the engine and hose cart. The horses, which wore neither blinders nor checks, were kept bridled day and night, the bits being taken from their mouths only when they ate their oats. They stood facing the apparatus, and when there was an alarm the doors of their stalls flew open automatically and the horses of their own accord rushed to their places with a tremendous thunder of hoofs on the wooden floor. The harness, which was suspended from the ceiling over their positions, was released when they were under it. The traces were kept attached to the whiffletree and the pole-straps to the collars. The girths were not used in dashing to fires. So all the men had to do was to snap the collars together and the reins to the bits. Meanwhile the driver had climbed to his narrow seat, fastened himself in with the safety strap, and in less time than it takes to read this paragraph they were off.

Training the horses was not a difficult task. A green fire horse was quick to understand what was expected of him when there was an alarm. Some learned with only a few rehearsals. Almost any horse could be taught in two weeks. There was usually an interested group outside a fire-house to see the horses dash to their places when the practice alarms were sounded at noon and at night. The best times to watch the horses do this was during the mild months of the year when the doors of the fire-house stood open, with only a rope stretched across the entrances.

In towns where the fire department was a volunteer organization, arrangements were often made with a liveryman near the fire-house to supply horses to drag the apparatus to fires, the town paying the liveryman each time his horses were used. The expense to towns for horse hire was not great, the bills as a rule not running over fifty dollars a year. If there was more than one livery stable in a town, the business was generally split up among them, each liveryman being given the job of furnishing horses for one or another of the different pieces of fire-fighting apparatus—the engine, the hose cart, and the hook and ladder. When the fire was close at hand the volunteers sometimes found the quickest way to get the equipment there was not to wait for the horses but to drag it to the fire by hand in the old way, which, of course, saved money for the town.

Liverymen occasionally complained that using a horse for fire purposes had a tendency to ruin the horse for ordinary livery work. A horse after a few years became so accustomed to going to the fire-house with all speed when the alarm sounded that there was danger that if it heard the alarm while being driven in the usual course of the livery business it would bolt for the fire-house.

With typical New England thrift, the city of New Britain, Connecticut, at one time used its fire horses on the municipal dump carts, and a fire there provided the citizens with a double feature—the dash of the dump carts to the fire-houses, followed by the rush of the engines to the conflagration.

In some towns which did not have regular fire horses no special arrangement was made with anyone to provide horses for the apparatus, but on an alarm of fire the first person to reach the fire-house with his horses received a fee from the town. In Spencer, Massachusetts, the sum paid was eight dollars, which many persons were eager to get, and whenever the alarm sounded there was a grand free-for-all race. Drivers of teams and wagons unhitched their horses and left their vehicles standing in the streets while they ran to the fire-house in the hope of getting there first and winning the eight dollar purse.

There is not much to be said about police horses. A few cities on special occasions, such as a presidential visit, mounted a few of their handsomest policemen on livery stable chargers and posted them at the head of the parade, but like the four admirals on horseback in the coronation procession of George VI, they usually looked uncomfortable, though their cab horse mounts were as a rule well behaved. Boston was about the only New England city which had regular mounted officers. Some of their horses were hired from livery stables. In 1892 a Boston liveryman was sued by a mounted policeman who was thrown and injured by a livery horse. The horse had been tried out and found suitable for police purposes before it was hired, but when the officer who was injured rode it on duty the horse became restive, shook its head, and ran violently onto a sidewalk, threw the officer, and then sat or fell on him, breaking his leg and otherwise injuring him. There was evidence that the policeman was an experienced horseman. There was no evidence that the liveryman knew or by the exercise of reasonable care could have known that there was anything about the horse which rendered it unsuitable for the purpose for which it was hired. The Massachusetts Supreme Court decided in favor of the livery-stable keeper, saying that one who lets a horse does not warrant that it is free from defects he does not know of and could not have discovered by the exercise of reasonable care. (Copeland *v.* Draper, 157 Mass. 558.)

The name Black Maria as applied to the closed police vans used to convey prisoners to jail is a term of New England origin, the story connected with it being that many years ago in Boston there lived a Negress named Maria Lee who kept a lodging house for sailors. It was a waterfront place in the North End, where brawls were frequent. Maria, who was a powerful creature, won a reputation for her ability to quell fights and bring the offenders to jail. So successful was she in handling tough characters that the police frequently enlisted her aid in bringing malefactors to book, and the story goes that when police wagons came into use, the police, remembering the help the Negress had given them, immortalized her name in the term "Black Maria."

Horse-drawn patrol wagons were not used generally in New England cities for many years after the Civil War. Drunken persons were carried to the station

house by patrolmen or were carted there in comman-
deered wagons or in wheelbarrows. One of the first, if
not the first, horseless patrol wagon to be operated in
this country was the electric vehicle purchased by the
Hartford Police Department in 1901. It was designed
after the standard horse-drawn patrol wagons then in
general use. A charging plant was installed in the
police stable and an extra set of batteries provided,
so that power would always be available for the wagon.
The running radius on one charge was twenty-five
miles and it could attain a speed of eleven miles an
hour. The chief drawback to the electric horseless
patrol wagon was that it made a loud buzzing sound
that could be heard all over town and was useless for
raids. One evening when it was called into service a
crowd gathered around it and showed its contempt
for the machine by good-naturedly tipping it over in
the street.

HORSE THIEVES

CHAPTER XII

Horse Thieves

Horse thieves were abroad at an early date in New England. In the seventeenth century a big gang of these pests was rounded up and tried at a special session of court held at New London. None was sentenced to have his neck stretched in a halter, but many of them were heavily fined and whipped. In 1785 Moses Parker was convicted at Hartford of horse-stealing and sentenced to ride the wooden horse for half an hour. To judge from contemporary accounts, riding the wooden horse was not much of an ordeal so long as the crowd refrained from pelting the rider with missiles. But riding the wooden horse was not the only punishment meted out to Moses Parker. He was, in addition, sentenced to receive fifteen stripes, pay a fine of £10, be confined in the workhouse for three months, and every Monday morning for the first month to receive ten stripes and sit on the wooden horse as aforesaid.

"Accordingly," runs the account in the *Connecticut Courant*, "the terrible machine was prepared—consisting of one simple stick of wood mounted on four legs; and by order of the sheriff placed on State House Square. Hither the prisoner was conducted, and being previously well booted and spurred by the officer, was mounted on the oaken stud. Here he continued for half an hour, laughing at his own fate, and making diversion for a numerous body of spectators who honored him with their company. He took several starts for a race with the best horses in the city; and it was difficult to determine who were most pleased with the exhibition, the criminal or the spectators. After this part of the sentence had been legally and faithfully executed, the culprit was dismounted and led to the whipping post, where the duties made him more serious. The whole was performed with great order and regularity."

David Aird, alias Charles Brewster, the Phantom Clockmaker of Connecticut, was another thief who was whipped and made to ride the wooden horse at Hartford for horse-stealing. He was "a trancient person apt to change his name, 5 feet & 8 or 9 inches high," with an impediment in his speech when he attempted "to speak quick." His method was to rent a shop in a town, advertise himself as a watchmaker and clockmaker from London, and after collecting all the watches he could, to abscond with them. Residents of Middletown, Connecticut, had occasion to regret his choice of that city for a temporary business location. " 'Tis supposed," said the *Middlesex Gazette* after

Aird had skipped town with a rich harvest of watches, "that he feels conscious of the wrong he does his native city by depriving it, by his absence, of so useful a member of society, and has returned again to London." But the *Middlesex Gazette* was mistaken. A year and a half later Aird paid a second visit to Middletown and stole two china-faced watches he did not get away with on his first visit.

George White was a notorious horse thief with a sense of humor. He once stole a horse from an innkeeper in Massachusetts and after thinning out the horse's mane and tail and dyeing its white feet, succeeded in selling the horse to the innkeeper from whom he had stolen it.   •

A prisoner at the Connecticut State Prison at Wethersfield who had charge of a pair of horses which were used at the prison became so attached to the animals that after his release he returned and stole them.

Mutual protection societies against horse thieves and robbers were organized in a number of New England communities. Two of these societies still exist in Connecticut, one at Enfield and the other at East Windsor, the former organized in 1833 and the latter in 1841. Needless to say, neither society has caught any horse thieves lately, the members now only being called on to attend the annual meetings and dinners of their respective societies, to which they drive in their automobiles. A newspaper photograph of a recent meeting of the Society for the Detection of Thieves and Robbers of East Windsor showed the president holding a small statue of a white horse, such as one sees in the windows of package stores to advertise a certain brand of spirits. The picture gave some people the impression that the members no longer quaff cider at their meetings but drink White Horse Whiskey instead.

Through the courtesy of Howard A. Middleton of Broad Brook, who has been secretary of the East Windsor society since 1894, I have read the leather-bound book, with marble-paper sides, in which the doings of the society have been recorded ever since the first meeting was held at the public house of Jonah A. Griswold on the evening of January 18, 1841. Children have drawn pictures in the book, which is now cracking at the joints, and once it was used to keep the record of a country auction, at which a candlestick was knocked down for 5¢, a pitcher for 25¢, a goblet for 10¢, a clock for $3.55, seventy bottles for 6¢ each, and a group of flatirons for 25¢. The book was easy to read, because the men who at different times have served as secretary to the society were in every instance good penmen.

Organized along lines similar to those of other anti-crime societies of the time, the constitution provides for a president, a secretary and treasurer, and a prudential committee of five directors. Provision is also made for "a suitable number of persons as pursuers to hold themselves in readiness each with a good Horse, to pursue forthwith on the shortest notice after any person or persons thereto directed by the committee."

Twenty-three persons were named pursuers at the first meeting.

"It shall be the duty of the committee or either two of them on complaint or information from any member of the society that His or Her Horse or Horses, Money, Goods or Property, that are situated or located within the limits of said society are stolen, forthwith to notify such number of the pursuers thereof as they shall think proper, and to employ any other persons to pursue if they shall think necessary, who shall without delay pursue after such Thief or Thieves in such way or manner as the committee or either two of them shall direct and each person at his return shall present his bill to the committee or either two of them who shall draw an order on the Treasurer for the same and each person shall be allowed fourteen cents per mile for their services, horse hire and expenses together with such sum or sums as they shall pay in passing any Toll Bridge, Turnpike Gate, & Ferries, computing half the number of miles actually traveled in going and coming."

Minors were encouraged to aid in detecting and tracking down wrongdoers and recovering stolen property by a promise of the same remuneration.

Anybody in town, apparently, could become a member by simply paying a dollar and signing the constitution. There were no dues, but in the event of an expensive manhunt it was provided that the society could assess its members. Money gradually accumulated in the treasury, and with true Yankee thrift the society loaned it at six per cent interest. As old members died and new ones joined and the society had no expenses, it began to declare dividends of two or three dollars a member, and the protection of the society was extended from time to time to fresh woods and pastures new, so that members could be recruited from a wider territory. Some years ago the society ceased loaning its funds and began keeping them in the bank.

"The trouble was," said Mr. Middleton, "the borrower had to lay the money on the table at the annual meeting and he never knew whether or not the loan would be renewed."

Although the society has existed for nearly a century, there is no record that it ever caught a horse thief. Once a man reported that one of his horses had been stolen, but it had only strayed from the barn. As may be supposed, the mere fact that the society existed probably afforded the community a certain measure of protection. That its purpose was largely of a preventive character is shown by the broadside which was printed and posted in all public houses in the area immediately after the society was organized. The broadside announced the formation of the association, "with a fund sufficient to apprehend and bring to Justice all persons who are guilty of Larceny within the limits of said society," and gave the names of the officers and pursuers.

There were, of course, no state police in New England during the horse and buggy age. Teletype machines were undreamed of and the radio was still a miracle of the future. But a horse, unlike an automobile, could not be driven hundreds of miles in a day

or night, and when a man's horse was stolen he knew
if he made the discovery within a reasonable time after
the theft that the animal was somewhere within a
radius of a relatively few miles. In attempting to
apprehend the thief and recover his property, he
followed much the same procedure as did a relative of
mine whose stable was plundered of a black horse one
night toward the tail end of the horse and buggy age.

This relative looked out of his window one morning
and saw that one of his horses had got loose from the
barn. He had a pair of horses named Tom and Jerry.
Tom was the lazy horse and Jerry the good one. It
was Jerry he saw cropping the grass beside the house.
He knew something was wrong, and going out to the
barn found that Tom and a brand new, small-wheeled,
rubber-tired buggy were missing. It was plain that the
thief had tried to get away with the pair of horses,
but that Jerry, the cleverer one of the two, had broken
away from him. The first thing my relative did was
to notify the authorities in all the surrounding towns
by telephone, supplying them with a description of the
horse and buggy and requesting that bridges be
watched. Then he went to the office of the local weekly
newspaper and had postcards printed describing the
stolen property and offering a reward. He sent the
cards to selectmen in a still wider circle of towns
throughout the state, with the request that the card
be posted in the general store or in some other conspicuous place.

The next day people began to call up from towns
on all sides to say that they had seen a black horse

and rubber-tired buggy. To judge from these reports, the thief was going around in circles on a grand tour of the state, but in reality people were mistaking other horses for the stolen one. This was apparent when the horse began to be reported in widely separated towns at the same time. Three or four days later, however, word came from a small town near the New York State line fully a hundred miles away that the horse and buggy had been recovered. A stranger driving a black horse and rubber-tired buggy had stopped in the town to buy oats for the horse. The buggy had attracted attention because it was new and smart and of a kind not seen before in those parts. The postcard had arrived only a short time before. There was no mistaking the fact that the stranger's horse and buggy were the ones described on the card. The man who sold the stranger the oats debated what to do. He let him start on his way and then overtook and stopped him on the road.

"Look here," he said to the stranger, "that's a stolen horse and rig you're driving. You come with me."

The thief made no answer, but standing up in the buggy as if to comply, suddenly threw a blanket over the other's head and leaping out of the buggy ran into the woods and disappeared.

RUNAWAYS

CHAPTER XIII

Runaways

Traffic in our streets before the age of motor-cars was in minuet time. Six or eight miles an hour was about the limit for horsed vehicles. Driving beyond that rate was unreasonable speed. There were specific ordinances against it. When trolley cars began to replace the old horse cars people talked apprehensively of their terrific speed and went for trolley rides just to get a thrill. But there were some people who for reasons of public safety were so opposed to the electrics, as they were called, that they would not patronize them. The first dead person I ever saw was a man lying in a welter of blood in the middle of Main Street in Hartford, a few minutes after he had been killed. This was one of our earliest street railway accidents and the town was horrified by it.

It was only in the most outrageous cases of reckless driving, where women and children were endangered, that the police took any notice. In the Nineties when the safety bicycle became the rage the main concern

169

of the police was the scorchers or speeding bicyclists. Many cities had squads of bicycle policemen with big mustaches who rode around in pursuit of these speeders. But there was one place where a person driving a horse absolutely had to go slowly, and that was crossing a wooden bridge. These bridges had to be taken at a walk. On most of them there was a sign which read, "Walk Your Horses." This was because fast driving across wooden bridges loosened the planking and made them dangerous to horses. It also cost money to repair them.

Crossing some of the long covered bridges, such as those which spanned the Connecticut River at Hartford, Enfield, Springfield, and Hadley, was tedious, and in summer the journey was hot and dusty, but there was nothing you could do about it, except to drink root beer out of stone bottles when you got to the end of the bridge. There were toll collectors stationed at many of the bridges whose function it was to see that you paid the toll and also made the passage of the bridge slowly. If your horse went faster than a walk, the fact was immediately known, for the sound of the horses' hoofs on the wooden flooring could be heard far and wide. One of my earliest recollections is on a still summer night hearing the noise of horses crossing the covered bridge over the Connecticut at Hartford fully a mile from my home.

There is a story told of a lawyer who defended a woman charged with fast driving across this same bridge. The woman was bringing garden truck to market, and thinking that she was late drove rapidly across the bridge and was arrested.

In court her lawyer said, "Your Honor, I submit there is no case against my client."

"Why not?" said the judge. "The law distinctly reads, 'No man shall drive across the bridge faster than a walk.'"

COVERED BRIDGE, WINDSOR, CONNECTICUT

To this the lawyer replied, "I still claim there is no case against my client. She is a woman and was driving a mare."

In the early days of the horse and buggy, news-papers sometimes pleaded with their lady readers not to drive alone for fear of accidents. But many women were excellent whips and managed horses quite as well as they did men. There were careless and incompetent

drivers then as there are now, but the horses had sense.
The kind of horses considered most suitable for
women to drive were those of the docile and gentle
variety, which in many instances simply meant that
the beasts were dull and stupid, the sort that, once
frightened, kicked everything to pieces and went dashing madly through the streets. Intelligent and spirited
horses might be quicker to shy and cut up, but they
were also quicker to understand and recover their
senses and not so apt to run away.

Newspapers of the period also had frequent occasion
to report stories of runaway horses, which often provided the only local excitement. The late Willie O.
Burr, owner of the *Hartford Times*, was known in
his early journalistic days as "the runaway reporter"
of his paper. Whenever a horse ran away he would
follow it up, find out who the owner was, and what
damage, if any, had been done. Another New England
journalist, John M. Bailey, widely known in the horse
and buggy days as "The Danbury News Man," often
wrote of runaways and seldom failed to get a touch of
humor into his reports. "An Adams' Express horse
becoming depressed by the corruption in Congress and
other high places, ran away on Monday and scattered
packages along the road. No damage was done."

But some of the Danbury News Man's stories were,
as he said himself, too good to be true, as, for example,
the following one: "An old Danburian, whose sneeze
is something like a thunderbolt, let off a charge on
Balmforth Avenue, Friday afternoon, near to a wagon
in which a farmer from Sugar Hollow was sitting

counting money. The horses were so startled by the
noise that they sprang forward, and started off at a
mad speed, leaving their owner floundering in the mud
and clutching desperately to a roll of scrip. The old
gentleman was amazed at what had happened, but he
was completely dumbfounded when the farmer rose
from the mud, and climbed a fence, and looked all
around. Then he came down and went up a tree. The
old gentleman thought he had struck on his head and
injured his brain. Pretty soon the farmer came down
from the tree, and drew a long breath, and said: 'It
must have been thunder, but I thought it was a gun.' "

Every town and city had its stories of freak runaways, of the odd and remarkable things done by
frightened horses, which were always running up on
porches, entering or trying to enter buildings, and generally getting themselves into fixes from which it was
difficult to extricate them. A horse is said to have run
at breakneck speed up the north steps and down the
south steps of the South Congregational Church in
Hartford without mishap. I cannot vouch for the truth
of this story, since it happened before my day, but as
a child I was dragged up those same steps to safety
by an older sister, as a runaway with a light sleigh
raced down Main Street and plunged through the
window of the drugstore on the opposite corner. The
horse came to a halt with its head in the square, old-
fashioned, black onyx soda fountain and was led out
through the front door not much the worse for its
experience. It was fortunate that this did not happen
at the next soda fountain down the street, where the wife

of the proprietor of the small confectionery store owning the fountain indulged the quaint practice of giving
the baby a bath in the soda fountain sink.

The worst day in the year for horses was the Fourth
of July. No one who could help it drove a horse in town
on that day. The Fourth was then neither safe nor
sane. It was celebrated in the streets with cannons, shot-
guns, revolvers, and every size firecracker, from the
small, snappy, Chinese variety to the giant crackers,
which, if touched off under a barrel, blew it sky high
and all to smithereens.

Frightening horses by tossing lighted firecrackers
near them was considered legitimate sport. If your
horse bolted in consequence of a firecracker exploding
under its feet, you got little sympathy. You should
have known better than to take your horse out on the
Fourth. So most people stayed home and ate water-
melon and ice cream, and if they wanted to hear the
Independence Day oration and witness the balloon
ascension, or if in the evening they wished to attend the
band concert and fireworks exhibition in the park, they
went in public conveyances or walked.

How milkmen hated the day! There was no better
kind of wagon to figure in a runaway than a milk cart
filled with cans and bottles. Daring indeed was the milk-
man who drove his route on the Fourth of July without
a helper to hold his horse while he ran round to back
doors delivering milk. Yet the milkmen of my own New
England city and its vicinity were supposed to have
cavalry horses. At least it was said that the First Troop
of Governor's Horse Guards was composed largely of

milkmen who rode their own steeds, and the cry when
they turned out for escort duty or to participate in
a parade was, "Here come the milkmen!" Certainly
their horses looked like milk wagon horses, and some
of the troopers could have passed for milkmen, but I
am sure few if any of them were milkmen. My personal
acquaintances in the troop numbered a grocer, a
bookbinder, a postman, and a couple of sons of
butchers.

A conspicuous figure in the streets of the town at
that time was a man who was held up to all small boys
as a warning of the awful consequences attending care-
lessness in celebrating the Fourth. The man had no
arms, or rather only two short stumps, having lost
both arms through the accidental discharge of a can-
non. Despite being thus handicapped, he was able to
drive a horse about the streets by having the reins
strapped to the stumps of his arms. He always drove a
horse of unusually high spirits and people wondered
at his ability to control the animal.

Many runaways ended in tragedy for both man and
beast. People were run down and thrown from vehicles
and from the backs of horses, and the horses themselves
were often so seriously injured that they died or had
to be destroyed. In the olden days wayside stones were
sometimes erected to commemorate these New England tragedies. Many of them still exist. Perhaps on
a boulder rolled up out of the rocky bed of a fern-
lined brook the traveler will read that near that spot
Sarah Stocking, aged ninety-eight, was tossed from
her horse and was killed, or that Pantry Jones fought a

losing fight with his rebellious horses. And many similar occurrences are recorded on tombstones in old New England burying grounds. These inscriptions often tell much in little. In the cemetery at Montague, Massachusetts, for example, there is a stone bearing this brief but full story of tragic death:

"Elijah Bardwell, died Jan. 26, 1786, aged 27 years, having but a few days survived ye fatal night when he was flung from his horse, and drawn by ye stirrups 26 rods along ye path, as appeared by the place where his hat was found, and here he spent the whole of ye following severe cold night, treading down the snow in a small circle. The family he left was an aged father, a wife and three small children."

My grandmother had a narrow escape when the horse she was driving down Pomeroy Mountain in Southampton, Massachusetts, ran away with her. She had been using only one hand to drive, because with the other hand she was holding one of her sons, then a baby only a few months old, in her lap. Beside her in the buggy was one of her daughters, a little girl. It was a desperate situation on a steep and dangerous road, but putting the baby on the floor of the buggy and placing her foot on the long skirt of the baby's dress, my grandmother took both hands to the horse, which she finally succeeded in bringing under control.

The unsung heroes of the horse and buggy age were the spectators who rushed out to stop runaways. It took nerve to stand in the path of a frenzied horse at the risk of being trampled under its flying hoofs, lunging for the bridle or reins as the animal passed, and hanging on until it could be stopped. Once, in a street crowded with women and children, I saw a policeman grab the bridle of one of a pair of galloping draft horses and after being dragged for some distance bring the animals to a standstill. On another occasion I saw a driver who had lost control of his horse when the reins broke leap from his carriage to the runaway's back and stop the horse. It was as good as a movie. Some people jumped from their carriages and wagons when their horses were running away, and probably more lives and limbs were lost in that way than by remaining in the vehicles.

A horse which ran away once, no matter from what cause, was likely to run again, and the advice of many of the horse and buggy writers was to take no further chances but destroy the animal. Those who had methods for breaking a horse of the vice were careful to instruct people to carry out the training in secret so as not to give the animal a bad reputation in the neighborhood.

THE HORSES OF NEW ENGLAND

CHAPTER XIV

The Horses of New England ·

THE first horse show in America was held at Springfield, Massachusetts, October 19, 20, and 21, 1853.
Weeks beforehand the countryside was plastered with
announcements in the form of three-sheet posters on
which were displayed a pair of horses' heads. A tract
of land near the United States Arsenal was enclosed
by a ten-foot board fence, a grandstand with 4,000
seats was erected, and a banquet tent and booths and
lunch stalls. Multitudes of people, including six governors in stovepipe hats, attended the show. Equally
distinguished were the equine guests. Four hundred and
seventy-five horses were exhibited. The show was a
wonderful success. The promoters put the profits into
establishing Hampden Park, where a mile track was
constructed. The park, which was opened in 1857 with
the blessing of Henry Ward Beecher, who delivered the
dedicatory address, became the scene of many stirring
turf battles.

Sixty years before the Springfield show a horse

was foaled—"folded" was the old New England expression—across the Connecticut River in West Springfield that was destined to become the foundation sire of the first notable family of American horses. The horse was Justin Morgan. Named after the schoolmaster who became his owner, the animal when two years old was táken to Vermont. There, between the time of his arrival in 1795 and his death in 1821, Justin Morgan laid the foundation of the Morgan breed of horses, which not only immortalized the name of his schoolmaster-owner but spread the fame of Vermont all over the earth.

Extremely interesting is the story of this remarkable horse. Absolutely nothing is known for certain about either the sire or the dam of Justin Morgan, though romantic stories have been told to account for the animal's origin and the amazing qualities which he transmitted to his descendants. One of these stories which received wide credence for many years was that Justin Morgan was sired by an English thoroughbred named True Briton, which according to legend was stolen during the Revolution from James DeLancey, an importer of English race horses in New York. But unfortunately for this story, DeLancey sold his horses and left the country before the war, and at no time did he own a horse named True Briton. There was, however, another James DeLancey, a colonel in the British army, from whom one Lieutenant Wright Carpenter of the American army stole a horse, which he rode into the American lines at White Plains. This horse was said to have been sold to Joseph Ward of Hartford,

Connecticut, who sold it to Selah Norton of East Hartford. Nobody knows, however, whether or not the stolen horse was True Briton, though it is certain that Selah Norton owned True Briton and that he bought the horse from Ward. True Briton also went under the names of Beautiful Bay and Traveller.

Now Justin Morgan the man was a school teacher in West Springfield, who in order to augment his earnings as a teacher made a business of standing stallions for public service. He also gave singing lessons and at one time kept a tavern in the town. He was born in the vicinity of Springfield in 1747 and took up teaching because in his youth he showed symptoms of tuberculosis, which precluded him from doing heavy manual labor. The stallions which he stood for hire were not owned by him. He would procure a stallion for a season under some arrangement with the owner for splitting the stud fees. In 1784 he had True Briton in West Springfield. A few years later, when he moved with his family to Randolph, Vermont, where he taught school and gave singing lessons, he continued standing other people's stallions for service.

In 1795 he told friends he was going to West Springfield to collect a debt. He was gone all summer, and when he returned he was leading a three-year-old gelding and a two-year-old colt. The colt was the horse that was to bear his name and stand at the head of the Morgan breed of horses. Justin Morgan said he took the gelding and the colt in discharge of the debt and that the colt was a Dutch horse. This statement of the schoolmaster is one of the few genuine clues to the origin of the horse Justin Morgan. It is known that a Dutch horse named Young Bulrock was standing in Springfield during the season of 1792, when the Morgan horse was gotten, and while it cannot be stated definitely that this Dutch horse was the sire of the colt taken to Vermont in 1795, it is quite possible that it was. The claim that True Briton was the sire evaporated when it was shown that in the season of 1792 the Connecticut horse was standing in East Hartford.

The schoolmaster did not live long enough to see his colt develop into one of America's most distinguished horses. Nor did he have any inkling that his name would go down in history as a result of his association with the horse. His wife had died in 1791 after giving birth to their fourth child and her death broke up the Morgan home. Neighbors adopted the children. Three years after taking the colt to Vermont, Justin Morgan died, penniless, in the house of a friend.

In 1857 a history of the Morgan family by D. C. Linsley was published which contained the following description of the foundation sire: "The orginal, or Justin Morgan, was about fourteen hands high, and weighed about nine hundred and fifty pounds. His color was dark bay with black legs, mane, and tail. He had no white hairs on him. His mane and tail were coarse and heavy, but not so massive as has been sometimes described; the hair of both was straight, and not inclined to curl. His head was good, not extremely small, but lean and bony, the face straight, forehead broad, ears small and very fine, but set rather wide apart. His eyes were medium size, very dark and prominent, with a spirited but pleasant expression, and showed no white round the edge of the lid. His nostrils were very large, the muzzle small, and the lips close and firm. His back legs were perhaps his most noticeable points. The former was very short; the shoulder blades and his hip being long and oblique and the loins exceedingly broad and muscular. His body was rather long, round, and deep, close ribbed up; chest deep and wide, with the breast bone projecting a good deal in front. His legs were short, close jointed, thin, but very wide, hard, and free from meat, with muscles that were remarkably large for a horse of his size, and this superabundance of muscle exhibited itself at every step. His hair was short, and at almost all seasons soft and glossy. He had a little long hair about the fetlocks, and for two or three inches above the fetlock on the back side of the legs; the rest of the limbs were entirely free from it. His feet were small but well shaped, and he was in every respect perfectly sound and free from any sort of blemish. He was a very fast walker. In trotting his gait was low and smooth, and his step short and nervous; he was not what in these days would be called fast, and we think it doubtful if he could trot a mile much within four minutes, though it is claimed by many that he could trot it in three."

By 1870 the Vermont Morgans had spread into every state and territory of the Union. Their smooth, natural trotting gait, their sure-footedness, and unusual powers of endurance, coupled with their intelligence, good manners, and quick style of action on the road made them great favorites. As general utility

horses they were unbeatable. Readers brought up on
The Youth's Companion will perhaps recall reading
some of its horse stories with their weight-pulling con-
tests in which the doughty little Morgan always licked
the big Percheron. But quite apart from the merits
inherent in the Vermont Morgans, there were other

A MORGAN HORSE

factors which contributed to their rapid rise in popular
esteem and to the large demand that was made for
them. The improvement of roads paved the way for
light pleasure vehicles, and for these vehicles a new
kind of horse was needed. Vehicular travel over the
old, rough, partly-improved roads was at a snail's pace.
In many places the rate of progress was barely four
miles an hour. Light carriages and wagons were useless

on such roads and speed was out of the question. The long hauls to market and the heavy going required big heavy horses. Progress in road-building and the improvement of agricultural implements gradually lightened the work of horses. Oxen and the large, round, slow draft horses began to be replaced by smaller and faster horses. The coming of the railroads proved a stimulus to horse-breeding. After riding in a train at thirty or forty miles an hour a man was not content to go five or six miles an hour behind a horse. He demanded one that would step off easily at an eight or ten mile clip. The Morgan horse answered his requirements better than any other horse on the market.

Testimony to the tough and lasting qualities of the Morgan breed is contained in the following letter written in 1892 to the editor of the *American Horse Breeder*:

"I am an old man, eighty-three this month, and seeing an article in praise of the Morgan Horse, I want to add a word of gratitude for their noble service done me as stage proprietor on the Fourth New Hampshire Town-Pike; as liveryman and farmer. For endurance, intelligence and as trappy drivers, the Morgans have no equals. To handle six or eight horses on a stage coach over hills—without accidents—looks to me wonderful now, for brakes were not known in those days. I sometimes think it could not have been done without the Morgan horse, for their superior intelligence was often displayed in cases of danger— like running on icy, sidling roads, where every tug was needed, and the horses on the run, to prevent the coach from falling off the bank! I have often done this and seen others do it, and accidents were few. These horses seemed to know what was wanted and understood the danger as well as the driver. It was sometimes no easy matter to carry the mails through blinding sleet and heavy drifts, but I never had a Morgan horse look back to refuse me. They always faced the blast. If a double trip had to be made, the Morgans always did it and the long-jointed, over-reaching, interfering span of some other breed was kept in the barn.

"Yours,

"J. C. Cremer, Hanover, N. H."

According to W. A. Gocher, the Morgan horse, with the possible exception of the gaited saddle horse of Kentucky, is the only distinct breed of horse to be developed on this continent. But famous as Vermont and New Hampshire became for breeding this American horse, it was Maine that took the lead in the production of fast trotters. At one time Maine furnished practically all the trotting stock of any note in the country. The breeders of that state seem to have been the first to realize that ancestry counts in a horse and a fast horse is not just a happy accident. Standing about the state were such stallions as Drew, Knox, Morrill, Eaton, Brandywine, Rising Sun, Gideon, and Hampton, all sires of more or less prominent lines of horses which gave Maine its reputation for trotters. But the real foundation was laid in 1816 when a son of imported Messenger, the English thoroughbred, was purchased in the State of New York by Alonzo Hayward and taken to Winthrop, Maine. The stallion was called Winthrop Messenger. It was the daughters and granddaughters of this horse which were chosen to visit the stallions mentioned. In this way Maine built up its trotting stock. Two Vermont bred Morgans foaled in 1855 proved excellent speed-getters in Maine. They were General Knox and Winthrop Morrill. General Knox was a black horse bred by David Heustis of Bridport, Vermont. When four years old he was acquired by T. L. Lang of Vassalboro, Maine, who sold him in 1872 to Henry N. Smith, who kept him at Fashion Stud Farm in New Jersey until he died in 1887. Thirty-two of General Knox's sons and twenty-nine of his daughters were speed-producers. Other Maine horses, notably Young Rolfe and the champion stallion Nelson, are dealt with in the chapter on racing.

Many good and stylish carriage horses in Massachusetts were the colts of Bellfounder, an English stallion imported by James Boot of Boston in 1823. He was a bay horse of unknown pedigree, but of fine form, size, and action, his appearance indicating that he was nearly, if not quite, thoroughbred. It was said that in England he had trotted two miles in six minutes when three years old and ten miles in thirty minutes when four years old. It was also claimed for him that he had trotted seventeen and a half miles in an hour. He transmitted his characteristics to his colts uniformly.

The first New England horses came from Leicestershire in England and were landed at Boston and Salem in 1629-30. Before the end of the century they were an important item of export from the New England colonies to the West Indies, where they were exchanged for sugar, rum, molasses, and salt. Rhode Island developed a breed of horses known as Narragansett pacers. These natural gaited animals were fast and were popular as saddle horses with the planters in the Dutch, French, and Spanish sugar colonies. When everybody traveled on horseback the pacer was in heavy demand, but when vehicles came into general use it went out of fashion, and during most of the horse and buggy age the pacer was considered the poor man's horse. The West India trade suffered a severe setback during the Revolution and the Narragansett pacer finally became extinct. Little is known about this Rhode Island breed. Some people think it was of Spanish origin, while others believe it was like the wild Irish hobbies.

The vessels used in the West India trade were called Horse Jockeys. They were heavily built, from one hundred to two hundred tons burden, and were slow sailers. They were rigged as sloops, schooners, and brigs. They made two or three voyages a year, timing their trips to avoid the hurricane season, and carried from thirty to seventy horses. For each horse an allowance was made of one puncheon of water (110 gallons), one bundle of hay (500 pounds), and ten bushels of oats. For handling the casks and hogsheads of rum, sugar, and molasses, which the West India traders brought back, a special vehicle called a Boston truck was used at New England ports. This was like a pair of skids on two wheels drawn by a pair of horses hitched tandem. With this curious contrivance, heavy loads were moved from the docks to the warehouses.

One day a Yankee skipper sailed into New London harbor after a long voyage from a South American port. On board his vessel was a colt slung up in a sling with three of its legs in splints. The horse was Ranger or Lindsey's Arabian, a Barb, which had been given to the Yankee skipper by the commander of a British man-of-war after the horse had met with an accident in a timber yard. A bashaw of one of the Barbary states had given the colt to the British naval officer, who had taken it with him to South America. Put ashore for exercise, the colt had been caught under a pile of falling timber, which broke three of its legs. The horse was about to be shot, when the Yankee skipper offered to try and save him. On the long voyage home the bones knitted, and when led ashore at New London the horse was sound.

"In a short time," says Mr. Gocher, from whose book, *Trotalong*, I have taken this story, "he became the property of Colonel Wyllys of Hartford. He called him 'Ranger' and advertised him for service in the *Connecticut Courant* in 1770. John Howard also had him in Windham in 1778, after which he was sold to Captain Lindsey and taken to Maryland. General Washington, who was a clever horseman, is credited with calling the attention of Captain Lindsey to this horse, his interest in him being aroused by the fact that he was the sire of many of the excellent horses in the Connecticut cavalry."

No less remarkable is the story of the horse Pilot, head of the celebrated family of that name. A Connecticut Yankee pedlar, Elias Rockwell, bought a fierce black stallion in Montreal for one hundred and fifty dollars. He got the horse cheap because of the animal's vicious character. He was able to manage him and brought the stallion to Stafford Springs, Connecticut, where he and the horse went into winter quarters. When Rockwell took to the road the following spring to sell Yankee notions the Canadian horse was tied to his wagon. He matched him in races along the way whenever an opportunity presented itself. At last the man and his beast reached New Orleans. Here the horse paced a mile under saddle in what was then the phenomenal time of 2:26. On the strength of this trial performance the peddler sold the pacer to Major O. Duboise for $1000. News of the time made by the stallion leaked out, however, and Major Duboise was not able to make any matches for the horse, so he sold him to D. Henisohn of Louisville, Kentucky, for just what he had paid for him. Pilot got Pilot, Jr., a gray horse foaled in 1844, who became a successful sire of racing material. A grandson of Pilot, Jr., was the noted trotting stallion Voltaire, 2:20¼. This horse was owned in Connecticut, the state in which its great grandsire had spent the winter before being taken to New Orleans by the Yankee pedlar.

In many of the rural sections of New England not much horse trading was done. When a farmer's horse wore out he usually had a colt to take its place. But if sufficiently provoked, few New Englanders could resist indulging in a little horse trading, and when they did you had to watch them, especially the deacons. For the Yankee was a born horse trader.

Pedlars like Elias Rockwell were always ready to swap horses on the road, and there were horse dealers who made it their business to drive about the country buying and selling by the wayside. New England had its gypsy dealers too. One tribe had its headquarters in East Hartford, Connecticut, for over fifty years. They spent their winters there and in the spring hitched up their vans and disappeared until autumn.

A classic story of New England horse trading is one told about the Vermont Yankee who set out from his home in the northern part of the state driving a sorry nag hitched to a decrepit buggy. At the first opportunity he swapped the horse and buggy and then traded again and again as he proceeded southward through his native state. When he reached Brattleboro he was driving a fine span of horses hitched to a splendid new carriage.

HORSE-RACING IN NEW ENGLAND

CHAPTER XV

Horse-Racing in New England

To tell the full story of horse-racing in New England during the horse and buggy age would require a folio the size of Cotton Mather's *Magnalia*. All that can be done in a single chapter is to give a brief sketch of a few of the main events in what is really a brilliant epoch in American turf history. The trotting horse was distinctly an American development and light harness racing a truly nationalistic sport.

Throughout the period New England was a great center of this activity.

Boston was the scene of the first public trotting race in this country. In 1818 a Maine horse, Boston Blue, trotted a mile in three minutes, which was considered a remarkable performance. Nearly eighty years were to elapse before a horse was to be driven to harness in less than two minutes. For decades men speculated as to whether or not it was possible to breed and train a horse that could trot or pace a mile under two minutes.

To produce such a performer was the bright particular dream of horsemen, but most people, including prominent breeders, trainers, and reinsmen, thought it would never be anything but a dream.

Then an important event occurred. This was the introduction of the bicycle sulky. On June 8, 1892, Charles Clark, who had a pacer, Alfred D., entered in a race at Worcester, Massachusetts, brought out a sulky equipped with a pair of ball-bearing bicycle wheels. Clark's horse won the race. Within a year the low-wheel sulky had displaced the old high-wheel style, and reduced the time of harness horses from five to seven seconds. Until then the greatest speeds were Sunol's record of 2:08¼ for trotters and Direct's pacing record of 2:06. The bike sulky brought the dream of the two-minute horse within the realm of reality.

Five years, however, were to pass before this became an accomplished fact. The first man to drive a horse under the two-minute mark was Dave McClary, who performed the feat at Readville, Massachusetts, on August 28, 1897, when he drove the pacing stallion, Star Pointer, around the mile oval in 1:59¼. It was one of the most sensational events of the century. The following contemporary account of the historic performance is taken from an old horse publication, *The Trotter and Pacer* for September 1, 1897:

"The day was perfect for record breaking. Not a breath of air was stirring when at four o'clock the horse came out with a running horse to make a trial for a world's record. The first two scores were not satisfactory to Reinsman McClary, and he worked the horse 'way down below the turn. But the third time down there was no hesitancy.

"McClary nodded for the word and off the pair went, the runner right at the saddle. It was an anxious first quarter for the friends of the horse, who all winter long, while he was owned in Boston, knew that all that was needed to wipe out the two-minute mark was to let Star Pointer's head loose. The first quarter was at an even two-minute gait in 30 seconds, and then as McClary called on the biggest of the free-for-all pacers to move the second quarter there was a great cheer, for he was beating two minutes all to pieces and got to the half in 59¾ seconds. Could he keep it up? Yes, and more, for the third quarter was the fastest of the mile. The distance was covered in 29¼ seconds at 1:57 gait.

"Around the turn Pointer seemed to waver for the smallest fraction of a second; but McClary had the fellow right almost before you could see it, and then as they straightened into the stretch the runner moved up even closer. Both pacer and runner were asked to step along. McCarthy laid the whip on the runner, but McClary said little to his horse save a word of encouragement. At the draw gate Star Pointer was reefed a little, and coming stronger from a distance, the greatest pacing stallion in the world appeared to freshen in the last few strides, gathered fresh strength and courage as he neared the wire and finished like a lion.

"A mighty shout went up, for thousands knew that a performance had been made to harness the like of which was never witnessed before in the annals of the turf. Hats were off, men yelled as though possessed. In the grand stand the owner had his hand wrung until it was nearly off. Over the fence jumped the men who knew horse and driver. Hardly had McClary got the horse to a standstill before they had him on their shoulders and he was borne down the stretch to the judges' stand, and, as the band played *Hail to the Chief*, he was introduced to the throng. A tip of the hat and then renewed applause for the horse, owner and trainer rang out in the dull air. A fairer mile was never timed. Not a watch in the stand but that agreed with the time announced, while on the other side of the stretch the grand standites caught it equally fast or faster. Not one slower."

Two of Star Pointer's shoes, a front shoe and a hind shoe, hang on the wall of Dave McClary's home in Hartford. On the same wall is a photograph of Star Pointer being driven by Mr. McClary in a race against Joe Patchen at Washington Park, Chicago. It is an enlargement from the first motion picture ever made of a horse race.

"I understand the original film is in the Smithsonian," Mr. McClary told me.

"How did you happen to become a trainer and driver of race horses?" I asked.

"The two-minute fever was strong in the agricultural community in Canada where I was born. People today can't realize how strong that fever was fifty or sixty years ago. I caught it bad."

"Is Star Pointer the best horse you ever drove?"

"Star Pointer had a fine disposition, but I always

thought Guinette, the horse I drove before Star Pointer, was a better horse," he said.

Another notable New England racing event is recorded on the monument over the grave of the famous mare, Goldsmith Maid, near the fair grounds at Trenton, New Jersey. The Maid made the best record of her career at Mystic Park, Boston, in 1874. The inscription on the stone marker reads:

HERE LIES

GOLDSMITH MAID

GREATEST AMERICAN TROTTER

QUEEN OF TROTTERS SEVEN YEARS

BORN SUFFOLK CO. 1857

DIED HERE SEPTEMBER 23, 1885

BEST RECORD 2.14 MADE AT BOSTON, 1874

EARNED $364,200 THE WORLD'S RECORD

DRIVEN BY BUDD DOBLE

OWNED BY HENRY N. SMITH

ERECTED BY

JOHN C. KUSER

1926

Budd Doble, named on the monument as Goldsmith Maid's driver, is mentioned by Oliver Wendell Holmes in his humorous ballad, *How the Old Horse Won the Bet*. And it was Budd Doble who drove the champion Dexter in the great race with Ethan Allen and running mate at Fashion Course, Long Island, June 21, 1867. Although it was known that a running mate was of great assistance, yet Ethan Allen, the champion New England Morgan stallion, was not considered in the

same class with Dexter, because even with the help of
a running mate his best time was slower than Dexter's
2:18 1/5, and he was not thought to have Dexter's endurance. The race excited a great deal of interest and
the result was considered entirely unprecedented.
Ethan Allen won in three terrific heats in 2:15, 2:16,
and 2:19, as against Dexter's 2:17, 2:18, and 2:21.
Ethan Allen's time, single, was never the equal of the
time made by Dexter in this race.

Both New Hampshire and Maine produced champion stallions, the former Fearnaught and the latter
Nelson. Like Ethan Allen, Fearnaught was a Morgan
horse. He was a chestnut foaled in New Hampshire.
His record of 2:23¼ was made in a $10,000 race at
Buffalo in 1868. It was the largest purse that had been
offered for a trotting race and the contest attracted
much attention. Fearnaught was a handsome horse. A
man who saw the race said, "He started for the first
$10,000 trotting premium ever offered in America. It
was a grand occasion. From his pedigree I was aware
that he was an inbred Morgan. This fact heightened
my amazement at his highly finished form, for he looked
like Marion by Lexington out of Miriam by Glencoe.
In the sunshine he was a golden chestnut. He stood
full sixteen hands high, and his body ranged grandly
in proportion. His flashing eye was as proudly defiant
as Milton pictures Lucifer's. He must have been
severely drawn for this eventful contest, for his chest
impressed me as unusually deep and capacious, his body
and limbs exceedingly lengthy, his flanks light and
tucked as a greyhound's, and his impatient eagerness

as great as Lancaster's when he made the fastest two-mile run on record." Colonel H. S. Russell bought Fearnaught for $25,000 and placed him in the stud at Home Farm, Milton, Massachusetts, where the stallion died in 1873. Some of his get were fast horses and a number of his sons and daughters were speed producers.

Maine's champion stallion, Nelson, was a bay horse, carrying Morgan blood, who was bred and owned by Charles H. Nelson of Waterville, Maine. Foaled in 1882, Nelson made his championship record at Cambridge City, Indiana, October 21, 1891, by trotting a mile in 2:10¾. "In some respects," says Mr. W. A. Gocher, secretary of the National Trotting Association, "he was the most remarkable performer ever foaled. From birth Nelson was a trotter and notwithstanding the handicap imposed on him by the manner in which he was trained and raced, he reduced the stallion record from 2:12 to 2:10¾, while he afterwards equalled the 2:10 of Allerton, when the resolute son of Jay Bird entered the list as a champion, and continued until he reduced his mark to 2:09. The match between this pair at Grand Rapids on October 8, 1891, brought out more people than were ever seen at a horse race in Michigan. Nelson was called the Northern King. In form, gait, and poise, either when in motion or standing, he was a superhorse."

Nelson's sire was Young Rolfe, a Massachusetts bred horse, which dropped dead during a race at Mystic Park, Boston, on September 18, 1884. Mr. Nelson, who had developed the horse in Maine, sold him in the

spring of 1884 to John Sheppard of Boston, who had
him trained for his first turf campaign, which up to
the fatal day at Mystic Park proved highly successful, with victories at Boston, Albany, Providence, Hartford, and Springfield, and good performances at
Rochester and Utica. Young Rolfe made his record of
2:21¼ at Springfield. He was the favorite in his last
race. He led the field until he had almost reached the
head of the stretch, when he suddenly broke and ran
wild, completely out of control. As he approached the
distance, Young Rolfe was seen to stagger and fall. He
died almost instantly where he fell.

A similar case occurred at Hartford in 1905, during
the race for the $10,000 Charter Oak Purse, when
Sadie Mac, heavily backed in the event, suddenly
dropped dead before thousands of her admirers.

It was Colonel Russell, the owner of Young Rolfe,
who in 1870 sold Ethan Allen (who retired from the
turf the year of his race with Dexter) to Amasa
Sprague of Providence. Amasa Sprague was the man
primarily responsible for the formation of the National
Trotting Association, which resulted directly from a
call he sent out late in 1869, inviting various trotting
associations to send delegates to a meeting in New
York. Forty-eight associations were represented when
the meeting was called to order February 2, 1870.
After two days' deliberation the meeting adopted By-
Laws and Rules for the National Association for the
Promotion of the Interests of the American Trotting
Turf. Later the name was shortened to the National
Trotting Association. It eliminated many abuses and

enforced discipline in the racing world. Since 1875 its headquarters have been at Hartford, Connecticut.

Prior to 1850 there were hardly any race tracks in New England, although Woonsocket, Rhode Island, had a mile track in 1849. Horse-racing was popular in Rhode Island even in Colonial times, and in 1749 a law was passed forbidding the sport under penalty of a fine of twenty-five pounds and forfeiture of the horse. In 1850 a track was built at Worcester, Massachusetts, which was followed in 1853 by Wyoma Park at Lynn in the same state. The Lynn road was a popular speedway long before there were any race tracks in the environs of Boston. One of the earliest race tracks in that locality was Riverside Park, which was followed by Beacon Park, Mystic Park, and Readville. In 1855 a mile track was established at Bangor, Maine, while the same year saw the opening of a half-mile track on Albany Avenue in Hartford, Connecticut, where a National Horse Fair was held the first season. The next year a track was built at Norwalk, Connecticut, and in 1857 Henry Ward Beecher delivered the address at the opening of Hampden Park at Springfield, Massachusetts. This park was on the bank of the Connecticut River and had a dike to protect its mile and half-mile courses. Hamilton Park in New Haven was inaugurated in 1859.

In 1860, tracks were constructed at Rutland, Vermont, Fitchburg, Massachusetts, and Belfast, Maine. Morley Trotting Park at Westfield, Massachusetts, came into being in 1863. Then there was a lull until 1866, when Brattleboro, Vermont, Foxcroft, Maine, and Manchester, New Hampshire, joined the list of track-owning communities. Among the tracks built during the Seventies were Agricultural Park at Northampton, Massachusetts, 1872; Oakland Park at Gardiner, Maine, 1873; the track at Brocton, Massachusetts, 1874, and the one at Keene, New Hampshire, 1875. In the last named year a lady owned Cocheco Park, the predecessor of Granite State Park at Dover, New Hampshire. Many other tracks were built in New England in the third quarter of the nineteenth century.

When racing at country fairs began in the Fifties it helped greatly to make trotting a popular sport. It also gave an enormous fillip to horse-breeding. There was not a town or village in New England without some enthusiastic persons, often farmers or the sons of farmers, who raised colts in the expectation of getting a ten- or twenty-thousand dollar trotter. The races at the fair grounds gave people a chance to see these home-grown products in action and the work of drivers whom they knew personally. The races also gave them an opportunity to see outside horses. Many of the trotters on the tracks of the agricultural societies were barnstormers on tour, some of them very much better performers than anyone suspected. For truth to tell, not a few of them were aristocrats traveling incognito —ringers on a round of the fairs. And just as performances on the big tracks established the values of fast trotters in the general market, so did events on the small tracks influence prices in the local field. Many a colt fetched a good price after coming in a winner in a hub-rubbing contest on his home track. But in spite of the beneficial aspects of racing, particularly the general improvement it brought about in the horse stocks of the country, to say nothing of the pleasure that it gave people, there was a great deal of prejudice against the sport, and the fair committees in many communities debated the question for a long time before finally deciding to erect a judges' stand and buy a bell.

The tracks built were usually half-mile tracks, at which the spectators have always enjoyed certain advantages not vouchsafed to the patrons of the mile ovals. The horses pass the grandstand twice each heat and they can be seen clearly at all times. It is true that horses cannot make such good time when they have to go two laps to the mile—it slows them down about four seconds—but the average spectator is more interested in close finishes than he is in time records.

Hampden Park at Springfield, Massachusetts, was the first New England track at which a Grand Circuit meeting was held. Springfield was, in fact, one of the charter members of the Quadrilateral Trotting Combination, which included Cleveland, Buffalo, and Utica. This organization developed into the Grand Circuit of mile tracks. The association's first season was that of 1873. Hartford followed Springfield's lead and joined in 1876, two years after the completion of Charter Oak Park. Providence was the next New England city to become a member. Its first meeting was held at Narragansett Park in 1883. After two more meetings in 1884 and 1885, Narragansett was out of it until 1899. Readville was not added until 1897. In 1898 Rigby Park at Portland, Maine, secured a date. But probably the best record was made by Charter Oak Park, where Grand Circuit meetings were held from 1876 to 1925, with the exception of the three years 1893, 1895, and 1896.

In the spring of 1937 this famous track was acquired by a corporation for an industrial site, and when I visited the park one evening late in May the grandstand was down, as were also many of the faded yellow stables under the trees along the backstretch. The buildings had been in a state of neglect and ruin for several years. The roof of the grandstand sagged dangerously and many of the boxstalls looked as if they were about to collapse. Few things look more forlorn than a deserted and abandoned race track. It is so easy to recall the spirited and colorful scenes once enacted there, the swaying crowd on tip-toe with excitement as the horses swing round the turn for the finish, and the shouts and cries as the final effort is made, that the contrast strikes one with something of a shock. Near the quarter-mile pole, which leaned drunkenly and was almost destitute of paint, I found Thomas Jefferson's grave. This race horse, known as the Black Whirlwind, is buried under a maple, to which one of his rusty shoes is nailed. Within a foot or two of the tree is a small marble marker bearing this legend:

THOMAS JEFFERSON

2.23

1863 · 1891

OWNED BY

WM. B. SMITH

A few hours before I found the grave, Dave McClary had shown me a photograph of this small black horse, with its long tail trailing on the ground. On the back of the picture someone had written, "Thomas Jefferson of Hartford, Conn. Had thrice earned record of 2:23. Started in sixty-one races. Won first money in forty-one. Won second money in nine. Won third money in five. Foaled May, 1863. Died April 17, 1891. Could not eat and was chloroformed. Never had a tooth dressed and lived to be twenty-eight." To which it should be added that two of the races which Thomas Jefferson won were $10,000 stallion races.

The owner, William B. Smith, was at one time a carriage-builder in Hartford, and the high-wheel sulky in which Thomas Jefferson won many races was made by the Mansuy and Smith Carriage Company. Not so many years ago the old sulky was resurrected and used in a parade. One of William B. Smith's sons was Winchell Smith the playwright, while Harrison Smith the publisher is his grandson.

The speed record of Thomas Jefferson may not strike one today as being remarkable, but he was a consistent performer, and it must be remembered that it took a long time to increase the speed of trotting horses from three minutes to two minutes. There is a stretch of many years between Boston Blue's record of a mile in three minutes made at Boston in 1818 and Dan Patch's performance at Readville in 1903 when he trotted a mile in two minutes flat.

Why, it may be asked, did New England breed trotters instead of gallopers? A gallop is a horse's fastest gait. It can run a mile several seconds faster than it can trot a mile. Why, then, inhibit the animal? It used to be said that it was partly a matter of temperament. The exhilarating ride in the saddle was not in harmony with the Puritan temper. It was tainted with incitements whose direct tendency was the race course, which was regarded with peculiar aversion. But it was only natural that trotting should be cultivated in New England when vehicles came into general use and displaced the saddle horse. A trot is the easiest gait for a horse in harness and the most comfortable for the driver. Naturally drivers competed with each other on the road. These impromptu brushes led inevitably to the establishment of trotting parks and to the organization of light harness racing, interest in which, it must be confessed, has waned somewhat since the horse and buggy age.

GLUE FACTORY

CHAPTER XVI

Glue Factory

THERE is a curious horse burying ground in Brimfield, Massachusetts, that is surrounded by a stone wall in the shape of a horseshoe. Oval stones represent the heads of the horse nails, while the calks are indicated by built-up sections of the wall. It is not a loosely constructed work. The stones are laid up neatly in cement and rest on a firm foundation. It was erected by a Brimfield man to mark the burial place of two favorite horses, Daisy and Jerry, which served him for many years. The space enclosed by the wall is forty feet across at the widest point, and other animals besides the two horses mentioned are buried there.

The horses of New England, like the people of New England, often lived to be very old, though life for a horse, with rare exceptions, ends before forty. The Brimfield horses, Daisy and Jerry, were ancients when they died. They were both over thirty-two years old.

A still older horse, a survivor from the horse and buggy days, was in 1934 enjoying a green old age in Plainfield Center, Massachusetts. This was Susie, aged thirty-seven, a black mare with two white feet and a white star on her forehead. Owned by the proprietor of the general store, Susie was known to walk up the three wide steps and enter the store when she saw her owner inside at the candy counter. On the road between Plainfield and Cummington, where a branch store was maintained, there was a sweet apple tree which Susie could not be made to pass in apple time without pausing to eat some of the fruit.

Like the owner of Susie, many people became so attached to their horses that when the animals had outlived their usefulness they pensioned them off and cared for them in their old age. A familiar object in the landscape of many a New England village was some ancient horse allowed to roam at large during its last years. There were no automobiles to disturb it as it wandered along the roadsides, and absent villagers inquiring for friends at home would ask also about the old horse.

Other people sold their aging horses, which in most cases meant condemning the animals to spend their winter years under unhappy or even downright wretched circumstances, perhaps between the shafts of a peddler's cart or a rag-picker's wagon.

A writer in the *Atlantic Monthly* suggested that there was an element of sternness or harshness in the Puritan character that made New Englanders unkind to their horses, but the only specific instance of unethical horse keeping which he cited was that of a skinflint, swamp Yankee who underfed his horses.

Many horses, of course, died publicly in harness, and I often wondered what happened to the body of a horse which had died in the street, but I never took the trouble to look into the matter. On more than one occasion I had seen dead horses carted away in the animal ambulance, but who was responsible for this or what was the ultimate fate of the body I did not know until a short time ago, when these same questions occurred to Cedric W. Foster, a reporter on the *Hartford Times*, who was curious enough to investigate and write a newspaper story embodying the facts which he unearthed. I quote the story to show the typical method of disposing of dead horses in New England cities.

"When we saw a horse lying on Whitney Street at Farmington Avenue Wednesday afternoon our curiosity was piqued. What becomes of horses that die in the street? In a rather vague sort of way we thought of the health department, the Connecticut Humane Society, the police department and the street department. Possibly they all entered into the situation. We even thought of a rendering plant. A little research has developed some interesting data.

"First, the horse must be removed by its owner. It becomes the duty of the police to locate the owner in the event he is not present when the animal dies. The owner makes whatever disposition he desires of the animal. If the owner is financially unable to remove the horse, the matter becomes complicated. He must hie to the welfare department and convince authorities there that he has not the funds to remove the body. If he passes this rigid examination the welfare department will issue an order on the street department calling for removal of the horse.

"The street department has no equipment for this work. The East Side Hide Company has for many years been doing it. Its vehicle for transporting the horse is specially outfitted with a ramp which may be lowered to street level. A rope attached to a windlass is then attached to the horse and the animal drawn into the machine. The body is then taken to the East Side Hide Company's plant.

"For many years it was the practice to bury the animals after salvaging the hides. But of late years there has sprung up a decided demand for horse meat in Connecticut, due to the number of fox farms in the state. Foxes thrive on this diet. So the salvage is now greater. Hoofs are utilized for glue and the hide may be used for many things. The tail is also of value.

"The old horse burying ground in Hartford was located partially on the site of the Dutch Point plant of the Hartford Electric Light Company. This plant was built about twenty years ago. During its construction the engineers ran into considerable trouble with the graveyard. The pits in which the horses were buried started originally at a depth of about twenty feet. The first animal would be covered with soil and later another horse would be placed in the same pit. These layers eventually reached within a few feet of ground level. After a number of years this section of ground was pretty well populated with the faithful animals that had trod the streets of Hartford and the burial place was changed to some distance back from the river.

"Ordinarily the forces of nature would have cared for the horses' bodies, but because of the dampness of the soil this failed to materialize. The fatty tissues, combined with lime and magnesium in the soil, formed a soapy substance which the excavators of the Dutch Point plant soon encountered. The result was that the workman felt like going on a strike. There was nothing to be done, however, except to finish the task and this was done as expeditiously as possible.

"In order to learn what became of horses the street, health and police departments were contacted and also the Connecticut Humane Society. One question could not be answered. That was: How long would a horse remain in the street when the owner was unable to pay for its removal and was in conference with the welfare department, the street department and the police department? No definite answer could be given. But it was agreed that some one of these organizations would take action. The East Side Hide Company would be called, officials said, and financial responsibility would be thrashed out in due course. The charge of the company for taking the horse away is ten dollars."

On another page mention was made of the grave of Thomas Jefferson, the black racing stallion, near the quarter-mile pole at Charter Oak Park in Hartford. The recent sale of the race track has made the preservation of the grave a matter of uncertainty. The question perhaps never would have arisen if, instead of being sold for an industrial site, Charter Oak Park had been purchased for the same purpose for which the race track at Clinton, Massachusetts, was bought in 1929. St. John's Church of Clinton acquired the old track there for a cemetery.

In the cemetery at East Hartford, Connecticut, there is a horse monument. It is not a memorial to a horse but to a horse dealer. Standing on top of a stone shaft is the bronze figure of a horse about two feet long. The work, which dates back to the Nineties, is signed by the sculptor.

One can do nothing but rejoice that the old New England village hearse is a thing of the past. In the early days people were borne to their graves on biers, while their age was tolled by the church bell. Hearses came into use when wheeled vehicles became common. In most towns the hearse antedated the fire engine. The right to purchase a hearse and to erect a hearse-house in which to keep it were among the implied powers of New England towns. Always a grim-looking vehicle, the village hearse frequently became so dilapidated that in the hilly sections of New England one could not be sure that in going up a steep grade the coffin would not come shooting out the rear end.

"We had two hearses, both of them one-horse," said the Rev. Charles L. Goodell, in his reminiscences of other days in the town of Dudley, Massachusetts. "The hearse house was built in the corner of the graveyard. We kept the old hearse there. The new one was in the barn of the man who conducted the funerals and saw that the graves were dug. The new hearse had four carved urns on it and draped white curtains on the side and end windows. It seemed rather interesting to us children that some day we might ride in state in the new hearse and perhaps they would give it a new coat of varnish that spring. Who could tell! When the new hearse came the old one passed to desuetude quickly. It was a thing to make a death bed terrible. The last promise exacted by more than one was, 'Don't let them use the old hearse for me!' It had no carvings and no windows. It was but a little advance over a drygoods box on wheels. It was dull black, where it had not turned gray like the hair of most of those it bore to their long home. Old Jacob said: 'Bury me not in Egypt,' but our people said, 'Bury me where you please but don't use the old hearse.' "

Fortunately, most of the dismal New England village hearses have moldered away since the passing of the horse and buggy age.

Acknowledgment

It is impossible to thank all those who have helped
me with suggestions and material for this book. In
addition to those mentioned in the text, I am under
heavy obligations to a number of booksellers and
librarians. Roger Johnson, bookseller and horseman of
Springfield, Massachusetts, loaned me books, pam-
phlets, and other material from his personal collection.
Crompton T. Johnson of Hartford let me use his book-
shop, in which there is a fine collection of New England
town histories, as if the place were a library, and my
old colleague in the book business, Lewis H. Stedman,
was generous of his aid. Mrs. Irene J. Smith of the
Reference Room of the Hartford Public Library found
material for me which I should never have been able
to discover for myself. Albert L. Bates of the Connecticut Historical Society also aided me materially, as did
the staff of the Atheneum at Westfield, Massachusetts.
Miss Anna L. Bates of the Hartford Public High
School and Miss Florence N. Blumenthal of the Avery
Memorial were helpful.

My thanks are due to Mrs. Mary J. Maher of Hartford for information about her son Danny Maher, the famous jockey, to W. A. Gocher, secretary of the National Trotting Association, who not only answered many questions but gave me leave to quote from his books, *Trotalong*, *Pacealong*, and *Racealong*, and to Herbert Finlay, the Hartford printer, for the loan of scrapbooks assembled by his mother, the late Mrs. James Finlay.

I gratefully acknowledge the interest and assistance of Frank J. Donaghue, J. Kenneth Bolles, James M. Strong, E. Welles Eddy, Thomas B. Hooker, and the late Cedric Ellsworth Smith.

Besides the members of my own immediate family, a number of other relatives have also been extremely helpful, especially Miss Annetta Clark of Smith College and Henry Eno Sage of Hartford.

I wish to thank the heirs of the late Charles Platt for allowing me to reproduce his etching of the covered bridge which spanned the Connecticut River at Hartford for the end-papers of this book.

E. V. M.

INDEX

223

INDEX

225

Concord wagons, their fame, 17, 18

Connecticut Courant, story of the punishment of Moses Parker for horse-stealing, 160; 191

Connecticut Humane Society, 215, 217

Connecticut State Prison, prisoner steals horses, 161

Cook, G. & D., first to apply mass production in carriage-building, 24, 25

Corsets, in the days of, 14

Country fairs make trotting popular sport, encourage horse-breeding, 206

Courting buggy, 107

Covered bridges, burning of one, 145, 146; their discomfort in summer, 170

Cummings, Josiah, harness and trunk maker, 38

Cummington Cattle Show, 72

Currier & Ives print, 137

Custer's Last Stand, favorite picture in saloons, 99

DALY, Father Bill, trainer of jockeys, 52

Daly, Mike, horse trainer, 52, 53

Dam break causes disaster in Williamsburg, Mass., 93

Dan Patch, his mile trot, 209

Dead horses, their disposal, 215; hoofs and hide utilized, 210

DeLancey, James, importer of English race horses in New York, 182

DeLancey, Col. James, of the British army, 182

Derby, Lord, 55

De Tocqueville, Alexis, mentioned, 47

Dexter, his losing race with Ethan Allen, at Fashion Course, 201, 202, 204

Dillon, Charles, owner of a New England hearse, 3

Direct, his pacing record, 198

Doble, Budd, race horse driver, 201

Dog-fights as a sport, 113

Dow & Gillett, whip-makers, 66

Downing, Lewis, originator of

Concord vehicles, sells his first Concord wagon, 18; his record of business, his retirement, 19, 20

Drake, Samuel Adams, his story of the Newport spectacle, 14

Drew, Maine trotting stallion, 188

Duboise, Major O., buys stallion Pilot from peddler, sells him to D. Henisohn, of Louisville, 192

Dudley, Mass., Rev. Charles L. Goodell's reminiscences of the town, 218, 219

Dwight, Josiah E., harness-maker in Concord, 39

EAST SIDE HIDE CO., its disposal of dead horses, 21, 217

Eating too fast in a horse cured, 106

Eaton, Maine trotting stallion, 188

Eaton, Henry J., chief of the Hartford Fire Department, 147

Election returns, methods of gathering, 5, 6

Emerson, Ralph Waldo, his fee for lecturing, 103

Emery, George H., harness-maker in Concord, 39

Empire State Express, mentioned, 147

Ethan Allen, wins race against Dexter at Fashion Course, 201, 202; sold by Col. Russell, 204; a model for weathervanes, 137

Express business, its early start and regulation, 117

FARES in hacks regulated, 114

Farnham, D. L., made first plaited whip, 63

Farragut, Admiral David, cruise around the world, 124

Fashion Course, Long Island, 201

Fashion Stud Farm in New Jersey, 189

Fearnaught, story of his $10,000 race, 202; placed in stud, 203

Fire horses, their character and quality, 148, 149; their training, care and manipulation, 152; hired from livery stables, 153